THIRTY SHORT COMEDY PLAYS FOR TEENS

Plays for a variety of cast sizes

LAURIE ALLEN

mp
MERIWETHER PUBLISHING LTD.
Colorado Springs, Colorado

Meriwether Publishing Ltd., Publisher
PO Box 7710
Colorado Springs, CO 80933-7710

Editor: Arthur L. Zapel
Assistant editor: Audrey Scheck
Cover design: Jan Melvin

Library of Congress Cataloging-in-Publication Data

Allen, Laurie, 1962-
  Thirty short comedy plays for teens : plays for a variety of cast sizes / by Laurie Allen. p. cm.
  ISBN-13: 978-1-56608-143-6 (pbk.)
  ISBN-10: 1-56608-143-2 (pbk.)
  1. Young adult drama, American. I. Title.
PS3601.L4324T48 2007
812'.6--dc22
                        2006035104

1   2   3   07   08   09

Table of Contents

Preface

The energy, excitement, and creative minds of teens have drawn me into their world. In this world, I have been inspired to create realistic situations where laughter emerges. The characters are often uninhibited, dramatic, unique, and full of ideas as they join their quest for experiencing life in a venturesome way. Their dilemmas become a way to act crazy, push boundaries, take chances, explore opportunities, and find laughter in a world of their own.

There are no complex issues to deal with and no lessons to learn. Instead, young actors will have the opportunity to entertain audiences as they show off their talents and do what teens love to do best — laugh! Students will delight in portraying the outrageous characters and unusual situations that develop naturally. They will be further encouraged as laughter is heard from their peers as well as the audience.

These thirty comedy plays can be used for classrooms, in competitions, and for an evening of entertainment. All the plays require few props, making staging quite simple. The true-to-life dialogs and contemporary situations enable students, actors, and the audience to relate easily to the material. This collection of short plays is suitable for all ages.

Plays for Two Actors

Pink

Cast (2 Male): Bruce, Paul
Costumes: Paul is wearing a pink shirt.
Prop: A book.

1 BRUCE: Man, what's up with the shirt?

2 PAUL: Hey, girls love pink!

3 BRUCE: Yeah, maybe for their lips or backpacks or shoes or
4   ribbons in their hair, but let me clue you in, Paul, they don't
5   like it on a guy.

6 PAUL: No, no, that's not true. *(Holds up book.)* Look, I've just
7   finished reading this book, and it says that imitation draws
8   attention.

9 BRUCE: What? What are you talking about?

10 PAUL: OK, it's like this. If you're into collecting baseball cards and
11   you see me with a stack of them in my hand, what would you
12   do?

13 BRUCE: Well, I'd probably come over and strike up a conversation.

14 PAUL: Exactly!

15 BRUCE: Unless the guy was wearing a pink shirt!

16 PAUL: Look – girls will be drawn to me because they are drawn to
17   the color pink. It makes them feel safe, happy, and all gushy
18   inside.

19 BRUCE: Hey, man, look, I don't feel all safe, happy, and gushy
20   inside standing next to a guy who's wearing a pink shirt.

21 PAUL: No, you're not getting it. It's about drawing out the
22   attention of the girls. And because they are drawn to the color
23   pink, they will flock to me like puppies to their mother.

24 BRUCE: Like puppies to their mother? Look, man, I don't think
25   so.

26 PAUL: No, think about it! When girls are born, what color is the
27   blanket that they are wrapped in?

1 BRUCE: Pink.

2 PAUL: Exactly! And what color is that little bracelet on their arm
3   that they wear home from the hospital?

4 BRUCE: Pink.

5 PAUL: Exactly! And what color do mothers decorate their
6   daughters' rooms in?

7 BRUCE: Pink.

8 PAUL: Exactly! See? Since birth, females are drawn to the color
9   pink! *(Pats shirt.)* And, voilá! Come to me, baby!

10 BRUCE: Paul, you've lost it. This time, you've really lost it! A
11   woman wants a man! A strong, tough man who can save
12   her from the world. A man who will wrap his strong and
13   protective arms around her.

14 PAUL: I know.

15 BRUCE: And just how protected do you think she'll feel being
16   held by a man wearing a pink shirt?

17 PAUL: But that's my point! She'll feel like a newborn baby
18   swaddled in a soft, warm, pink blankey. *(Pats his shirt.)*

19 BRUCE: Blankey?

20 PAUL: Blanket!

21 BRUCE: So you're a soft, warm blanket?

22 PAUL: *(Opens his arms wide.)* Exactly! Like I quoted from this
23   book, "Imitation draws attention."

24 BRUCE: No, imitation is going to draw you a lot of laughs.

25 PAUL: I'll become a magnet to the girls.

26 BRUCE: *(Looking around, sarcastically)* I've noticed. Look, man,
27   lose the color and go with something more macho like
28   black or blue. I'm telling you, pastels, especially pink, are
29   not colors for a man!

30 PAUL: Bruce, women love pastels! And they'll love me in this
31   pretty color.

32 BRUCE: "Pretty color." Wow. Look, big guy, how many girls
33   have you run across with your, uh … new attention-
34   grabbing pink shirt?

35 PAUL: None yet, but I was on my way to the mall. See, that's

1   something else, women love to shop, so that's what I'm
2   going to do because as the book says ...
3 PAUL and BRUCE: *(Together)* "Imitation draws attention."
4 PAUL: It's like that saying, "Great minds think alike."
5 BRUCE: What about that saying, "Opposites attract"?
6 PAUL: Hmmm ... I haven't had any luck with that one. But
7   anyway, I'm going to do as this book suggests, and I know
8   it's going to work like magic!
9 BRUCE: Well, good luck.
10 PAUL: So, you want to come with me to the mall?
11 BRUCE: Nah, I'm headed to the paintball field. Real men need
12   to stay prepared when it comes to our survival skills. You
13   never know when we might have to go back to the days of
14   hunting down our next meal or fighting the Indians.
15 PAUL: Hunting for our next meal? Fighting Indians?
16 BRUCE: But hey, you have fun shopping at the mall. See ya.
17   *(Exits.)*
18 PAUL: Bye. *(He looks at his shirt and smiles.)* Look out, ladies,
19   here I come!

Third

Cast (1 Male, 1 Female): Grant, Andrea
Props: Tube of lip balm.
Setting: The school's roof.

1   *(AT RISE: GRANT and ANDREA are sitting down having a*
2   *picnic.)*
3   **ANDREA:** This was such a romantic idea!
4   **GRANT:** So you like picnics?
5   **ANDREA:** I love picnics! *(Laughs.)* But I have to say I haven't
6   had too many picnics on a roof!
7   **GRANT:** Well, I like to be original.
8   **ANDREA:** It's perfect. And look at all the stars!
9   **GRANT:** Uh ... I don't see any stars.
10   **ANDREA:** I'm pretending. Pretending that it's a warm summer
11   evening and the sky is full of bright, radiant stars. And the
12   moon is over there, big, round, full, and beautiful!
13   Glowing like never before!
14   **GRANT:** Wow. You do have a good imagination.
15   **ANDREA:** And I love being the first girl that you brought to the
16   roof. OK, so maybe it's just the roof of our high school, but
17   still, I feel special!
18   **GRANT:** Third.
19   **ANDREA:** Forget that we're eating yucky cafeteria food, forget
20   it's only a forty-five-minute lunch hour, and forget it's not
21   a dark, warm evening with the sky full of stars, but ... but
22   what did you mean? Third?
23   **GRANT:** Well, Andrea, you know I don't lie.
24   **ANDREA:** I know you don't lie, Grant. You've never lied to me.
25   **GRANT:** Well, you said you were the first girl I'd brought to the
26   roof, and that's not true. You're the third.
27   **ANDREA:** What? The third? The *third*? Who? When? Why?

1   GRANT: Becky, Teresa ... you know.
2   ANDREA: No, I don't know! I thought us coming up here to the
3   roof during our lunch hour for a picnic was, was ... you
4   know ... special!
5   GRANT: It is special!
6   ANDREA: How can it be special if you've already done it with
7   two other girls?
8   GRANT: Because I wasn't thinking about the other two girls.
9   You know, if this is ruined because I told you the truth,
10   then let's just go.
11   ANDREA: No, I don't want to go!
12   GRANT: Come on. The bell's going to ring anyway.
13   ANDREA: No!
14   GRANT: Why?
15   ANDREA: I want the truth!
16   GRANT: I told you the truth.
17   ANDREA: Why did you bring me up here for a picnic on the
18   roof?
19   GRANT: I thought it would be fun.
20   ANDREA: And romantic?
21   GRANT: Well, yeah.
22   ANDREA: Like it was romantic with Becky and Teresa?
23   GRANT: It wasn't that romantic with Becky and Teresa. In fact,
24   they didn't even like it up here. I was hoping you would be
25   different.
26   ANDREA: Oh. Oh. *(Smiles.)* Well, I am different! I do like it. We
27   should do this every day!
28   GRANT: Come on. Let's go back down.
29   ANDREA: No, I want to finish our picnic!
30   GRANT: Come on, Andrea. The bell's going to ring in a few
31   minutes, and we need to sneak down before we get caught.
32   ANDREA: No, let's skip all our afternoon classes and stay up
33   here on the roof! That way, I'll be the first girl you cut class
34   and hid out with on the roof.
35   GRANT: Third.

1 ANDREA: And we can finish our picnic and talk and ... What?
2   What do you mean, third?
3 GRANT: Well, Becky and Teresa both wanted to do the same
4   thing.
5 ANDREA: They had the same idea as me? But I thought they
6   didn't like the roof.
7 GRANT: They didn't after spending all afternoon up here. It
8   got boring.
9 ANDREA: But ... but ...
10 GRANT: Come on. Let's go back down before the bell rings.
11 ANDREA: But ... but what if we spent the entire time kissing?
12   That wouldn't be boring! And I could be the first girl you
13   brought to the roof and kissed as we skipped all our
14   afternoon classes!
15 GRANT: Third.
16 ANDREA: And I brought some lip balm. You want some?
17   *(Offering him lip balm)* What? What do you mean, third?!
18 GRANT: I told you, I don't lie.
19 ANDREA: Well, this is just great! And I thought I was someone
20   special! I thought we were doing something different!
21 GRANT: Actually, we are.
22 ANDREA: What?
23 GRANT: Not staying, not skipping class, and not kissing. *(He*
24   *smiles. She throws the lip balm at him.)*
25 ANDREA: Next time, try to be more original!

Blackout

Cast (2 Female): Sherrie, Melissa
Props: Two large purses or bags, extension cord, makeup, large mirror, cell phone, cellphone charger, curling iron, hair straightener, two drinks, snacks, hairspray, digital camera with charger, two textbooks.
Setting: A classroom.

1   *(AT RISE: SHERRIE and MELISSA rush in and sit down at*
2   *two desks. They each carry a large purse or bag.)*
3   **SHERRIE:** It's OK. Mrs. Shamblin didn't even notice that we
4   came in two minutes after the bell.
5   **MELISSA:** Mrs. Shamblin doesn't notice anything.
6   **SHERRIE:** Thank goodness. OK, tell me when she's not
7   looking.
8   **MELISSA:** She's not looking. You know, she's never looking.
9   So, why do you always ask me to tell you when she's not
10   looking?
11 **SHERRIE:** Just to be on the safe side, I guess. *(She takes an*
12   *extension cord out of her bag, gets up, and plugs it into an*
13   *outlet. Then she sits down, takes a hair straightener or*
14   *curling iron from her bag, and plugs it in.)*
15 **MELISSA:** *(Takes makeup and a large mirror from her bag.)* I
16   love having Mrs. Shamblin for first period. She puts our
17   assignment on the board each morning, and then reads
18   her romance novels.
19 **SHERRIE:** And all she expects us to do is answer the questions
20   at the end of each chapter. And lucky me, some nerd from
21   last year wrote the answers in my book.
22 **MELISSA:** *(Looking in the mirror)* And I appreciate you sharing
23   those answers with me, your very best friend.
24 **SHERRIE:** My pleasure.

1 MELISSA: *(Hands SHERRIE a cellphone and charger.)* **Here, I**
2 **need to charge my phone. Will you plug it in for me?**
3 SHERRIE: **No problem. I should probably charge my phone,**
4 **too.** *(They put on makeup and fix their hair.)*
5 MELISSA: **It's nice having first period to get ready in the**
6 **morning. It gives me extra time to sleep every day.**
7 SHERRIE: **Tell me about it. I hate mornings. Oh, I brought us**
8 **breakfast.** *(Digs into her bag and takes out two drinks and*
9 *snacks.)*
10 MELISSA: **Thanks! I'm hungry.** *(They eat and continue with*
11 *their hair and makeup.)*
12 SHERRIE: **Does my eye shadow look OK?**
13 MELISSA: **Yeah, it looks pretty. Can I borrow it? I want to try**
14 **that color.**
15 SHERRIE: **Sure.**
16 MELISSA: **My mom says I wear too much makeup, but what**
17 **does she know?**
18 SHERRIE: **I know, my mom says the same thing. "Why do you**
19 **put all that stuff on your face? Your skin is so young and**
20 **beautiful."**
21 MELISSA: **They want us to look twelve.**
22 SHERRIE: *(Looking at herself in the mirror)* **I'd rather look**
23 **twenty.**
24 MELISSA: **Me, too.**
25 SHERRIE: **Do you have any hairspray?**
26 MELISSA: **Let me check.** *(Looks in bag.)* **You're in luck. Here**
27 **you go.**
28 SHERRIE: **Thanks. You know, Mrs. Shamblin should try**
29 **wearing a little more makeup. She looks kind of plain,**
30 **don't you think?**
31 MELISSA: **Kind of? She needs a major makeover. Too bad she**
32 **doesn't look up and notice how well we do our makeup**
33 **and ask for a little help.**
34 SHERRIE: **Yeah, but if she looked up and noticed what we**
35 **were doing, I'm afraid we'd be in major trouble.**

1 MELISSA: Yeah, I guess. But she never notices anything.

2 SHERRIE: Thank goodness.

3 MELISSA: I really like this class.

4 SHERRIE: Me, too.

5 MELISSA: Thanks for the breakfast. It's good. Let's see ...
6   what's our assignment for the day? *(Reading off the board)*
7   Read chapter sixteen and answer the study questions.

8 SHERRIE: No problem. I have the answers and you can copy.

9 MELISSA: Thank you very much.

10 SHERRIE: Hey, that eye shadow looks good on you!

11 MELISSA: Thanks! I like it. Can I borrow your straightener?

12 SHERRIE: Sure. *(They continue with their hair and makeup.*
13   *MELISSA looks up and suddenly looks frightened. She*
14   *nudges SHERRIE, who looks up.)*

15 SHERRIE: Why is she staring at us?

16 MELISSA: I don't know. She never looks this way.

17 SHERRIE: I know. Just smile and look down as if you're
18   working on your assignment. *(They both smile and look*
19   *down.)*

20 MELISSA: *(Still looking down)* I hope she doesn't notice the
21   extension cord.

22 SHERRIE: Or the makeup. Or the cellphones. Or the breakfast.

23 MELISSA: Do you think it's good or bad that she's not saying
24   anything?

25 SHERRIE: Probably bad.

26 MELISSA: What are we going to do?

27 SHERRIE: I don't know.

28 MELISSA: Let's say we've never done this before ...

29 SHERRIE: That's a lie.

30 MELISSA: And we were both running late this morning
31   because ... because ...

32 SHERRIE: You picked me up for school and we had car
33   trouble.

34 MELISSA: And we went back home to get our makeup,
35   straightener, and an extension cord?

1   SHERRIE: Don't forget breakfast.

2   MELISSA: So why isn't she screaming at us?

3   SHERRIE: Or walking over here?

4   MELISSA: Maybe she's writing us a pass to the principal's

5   office.

6   SHERRIE: I bet that's it. She sure does write slow.

7   MELISSA: *(Slowly looks up.)* Hey, she went back to her reading!

8   SHERRIE: *(Looks up.)* You're right!

9   MELISSA: Guess she doesn't care if we spend first period

10   getting ready for school.

11   SHERRIE: Hey, she was a teenager once. She knows how it is.

12   MELISSA: Or maybe she wasn't even looking at us. Maybe she

13   was daydreaming about something in her book.

14   SHERRIE: I bet that's it. She was probably looking right past

15   us.

16   MELISSA: I'm sure that was it.

17   SHERRIE: Oh, well. Are you finished with the straightener?

18   MELISSA: Almost.

19   SHERRIE: Take your time. I need to plug in my digital camera

20   and let it charge. I want to take some pictures of Brad next

21   period. *(As she leans down to plug in a camera, the lights*

22   *suddenly go out.)*

23   MELISSA: What happened?

24   SHERRIE: Uh … I think I tried to plug too many things in at

25   once. I think I blew a circuit.

26   MELISSA: What are we going to do?

27   SHERRIE: I think we better put all this stuff away before the

28   lights come on and Mrs. Shamblin notices! Hurry, OK?

29   *(The girls rush around the room putting everything away.*

30   *They take out their books and are looking at them when the*

31   *lights come back on.)*

32   MELISSA: *(Looking up)* Can you believe that?

33   SHERRIE: *(Looking up)* What?

34   MELISSA: Mrs. Shamblin never even looked up from her book.

35   SHERRIE: What does she do? Read in the dark?

1   **MELISSA:** No, she just put a flashlight down!

2   **SHERRIE:** That is one weird teacher.

3   **MELISSA:** Thank goodness. But next time, don't try plugging

4   **so many things in at once.**

5   **SHERRIE:** Believe me. I learned my lesson. *(They go back to*

6   *doing their makeup and hair.)*

Class Clown

Cast (2 Male): Mr. Pruitt, Wesley
Props: Several paper airplanes, a textbook.
Setting: A classroom.

1   *(AT RISE: WESLEY sits in a school desk facing the audience.*
2   *MR. PRUITT stands in front of WESLEY and walks back and*
3   *forth as he speaks to a classroom.)*
4   **MR. PRUITT: The South produced more than half the world's**
5   **supply of cotton. And after the cotton gin was invented in**
6   **1793, cotton became profitable and more slaves were**
7   **needed.** *(As MR. PRUITT walks past WESLEY's desk,*
8   *WESLEY throws a paper airplane.)* **And although slave**
9   **importation was banned in 1808, slave smuggling**
10   **continued because of the high demand. And the life of a**
11   **slave meant hard work. If orders weren't followed,**
12   **whippings were given. And there were no civil or political**
13   **rights.** *(Again, WESLEY throws a paper airplane as MR.*
14   *PRUITT walks by.)* **Laws to protect slaves were often**
15   **difficult to enforce. And because of their bondage, slaves**
16   **had no dignity and were often illiterate ...** *(Again, WESLEY*
17   *throws a paper airplane, but this time it hits MR. PRUITT.*
18   *WELSEY looks away and attempts to look innocent.)* **Mr.**
19   **Hollis!**
20 **WESLEY: Sir?**
21 **MR. PRUITT: Did you just throw a paper airplane?**
22 **WESLEY: Me?** *(Shaking his head)* **No. Not me.**
23 **MR. PRUITT: Mr. Hollis, may I remind you that the reason you**
24   **are seated at the front of the classroom and away from**
25   **everyone else is because you can't behave! Do I need to**
26   **turn your desk around so you have to face the wall?**
27 **WESLEY: No. No, sir.**

1   **MR. PRUITT:** *(Holding the paper airplane)* **And do you think**
2   **this is funny? Throwing paper airplanes across the room**
3   **when I'm teaching my class? Do you?**
4   **WESLEY: Yes. I mean, no! I mean ...** *(MR. PRUITT glares at him.)*
5   **I mean ... OK, it was funny. But, I mean, to you, I'm sure it**
6   **wasn't funny.** *(Points to the classroom. Laughs.)* **But they all**
7   **thought it was funny, too.**
8   **MR. PRUITT: You know what, Mr. Hollis; I've had just about**
9   **enough of you! And do you realize that if you get sent**
10   **down to the office one more time you're going to be**
11   **expelled?**
12   **WESLEY: Yes, sir.**
13   **MR. PRUITT: And don't you think that you need an education,**
14   **Mr. Hollis? Or would you rather sit at home and watch TV**
15   **and play on the computer?**
16   **WESLEY: Honestly?**
17   **MR. PRUITT: Mr. Hollis, you are testing my very last nerve!**
18   **WESLEY: Sorry, sir.**
19   **MR. PRUITT: Do you realize how hard it is to teach a class**
20   **when you have one disruptive, rude, and immature**
21   **student?**
22   **WESLEY:** *(Smiles.)* **But don't you think that every class needs a**
23   **class clown? You know, add a little fun to the room?**
24   **MR. PRUITT: Oh, you think so?**
25   **WESLEY: Honestly ... yes.**
26   **MR. PRUITT: OK, then I have an idea. For a major grade in my**
27   **class, you can teach the class today.** *(Hands him a book.)*
28   **Chapter twenty-five. "The South and the Slavery**
29   **Controversy."**
30   **WESLEY: But ... but ...**
31   **MR. PRUITT: Stand up, stand up!**
32   **WESLEY: But ...**
33   **MR. PRUITT: And if you blow it, Mr. Hollis, it's a zero for you ...**
34   **and you'll be on your way to the principal's office!**
35   **WESLEY:** *(Stands.)* **But ...** *(MR. PRUITT sits in WESLEY's chair*

1   *and begins making paper airplanes. He also makes faces and*
2   *gestures behind WESLEY's back as WESLEY talks. WESLEY*
3   *flips through the textbook.)*
4 WESLEY: OK ... uh ... "The South and the Slavery Controversy."
5   *(He reads.)* Uh ... Slave importation was banned in 1808,
6   but smuggling of them continued due to their high
7   demand. By 1860 there were four million slaves. Uh ... in
8   1850, only one thousand, seven hundred and thirty-three
9   families owned more than a hundred slaves each.
10 MR. PRUITT: *(Throws a paper airplane.)* I'm confused! You're
11   skipping around too much, Mr. Hollis. Skip, skip, skip.
12 WESLEY: Uh ... It was 1793 when the cotton gin was invented.
13   And the, uh ... South was uh ... burdened with depressed
14   prices ....
15 MR. PRUITT: *(Raising his hand)* Can I go to the bathroom?
16 WESLEY: *(Looks at him, then looks away, not knowing what to*
17   *say.)* OK, it was 1793 when the cotton gin was invented ...
18 MR. PRUITT: You already told us that!
19 WESLEY: OK, uh ... it was invented by ... by ... Eli Whitney.
20 MR. PRUITT: *(Raising his hand)* What does that have to do with
21   the slaves?
22 WESLEY: I, uh ... don't know ...
23 MR. PRUITT: Can I go to the bathroom?
24 WESLEY: *(Looking at the book)* Cotton became more profitable
25   and more slaves were needed ...
26 MR. PRUITT: Are you going to let me go to the bathroom?
27 WESLEY: *(Looking at the book)* The South produced more than
28   half the world's supply of cotton ...
29 MR. PRUITT: Are we supposed to be taking notes? Are we going
30   to have a test on this?
31 WESLEY: So the South held an advantage over countries like
32   England, which needed cotton ...
33 MR. PRUITT: *(Throws a paper airplane.)* Can I borrow some
34   paper? Did you say we have to take notes?
35 WESLEY: *(Bolts around.)* Would you just shut up! *(Suddenly he*

1   *realizes what he's done.)* **Oh ... uh ... sorry, Mr. Pruitt.**

2 **MR. PRUITT: Are we supposed to be taking notes?**

3 **WESLEY: Uh ... yes.**

4 **MR. PRUITT: Oh! I didn't know! Then could you repeat what**

5   **you just said? Oh, and can I borrow a pen?**

6 **WESLEY:** *(Gives him a pen, then looks at the book.)* **OK, "The**

7   **South and the Slavery Controversy"** ...

8 **MR. PRUITT: How do you spell controversy?**

9 **WESLEY: It's in your book! Chapter twenty-five!**

10 **MR. PRUITT: Oh, OK. Hold on. Hold on. Let me find it. OK, I'm**

11   **ready.** *(As WESLEY speaks, MR. PRUITT throws numerous*

12   *paper airplanes at him and makes all sorts of funny*

13   *gestures.)*

14 **WESLEY: The uh ... cotton gin was invented by Eli Whitney in**

15   **uh ... 1973 ... no, not 1973, that was 1793. Yeah, 1793. And**

16   **after the gin was invented, cotton became more profitable**

17   **and ... and ...** *(Abruptly turns around.)* ***Would you stop it?!***

18   ***Please! I can't concentrate when you are doing that!***

19 **MR. PRUITT:** *(Smiles.)* **It wasn't me.**

20 **WESLEY:** ***Yes it was!***

21 **MR. PRUITT: Don't look at me!**

22 **WESLEY: Mr. Pruitt, you are really getting on my nerves! I'm**

23   **trying to teach this class! I'm trying to concentrate!**

24 **MR. PRUITT: Don't let me stop you.**

25 **WESLEY: If I could send you to the principal's office, I would!**

26 **MR. PRUITT:** *(Smiles.)* **But you can't.**

27 **WESLEY: Stand up!**

28 **MR. PRUITT: What?**

29 **WESLEY:** ***Stand up!*** *(MR. PRUITT stands up and WESLEY turns*

30   *the desk around to face the wall.)* ***Sit down!***

31 **MR. PRUITT:** *(Sits down.)* **But I don't like facing the wall! I feel**

32   **left out!**

33 **WESLEY:** *(Looking at the book)* **OK, it was 1973 ... no, I mean,**

34   **1793 when the cotton gin was invented.**

35 **MR. PRUITT: I don't like staring at the wall!**

1   **WESLEY: Yes, 1793 ...**

2   **MR. PRUITT: Can you talk louder?**

3   **WESLEY:** *(Loudly)* **It was 1793 ...**

4   **MR. PRUITT: What year?**

5   **WESLEY: 1793!**

6   **MR. PRUITT: 1973?**

7   **WESLEY:** *1793!*

8   **MR. PRUITT: 1793 or 1973?**

9   **WESLEY:** *(Angrily, he pushes MR. PRUITT's desk off the stage*

10   *then returns. Out of breath, he continues.)* **OK, it was 1973**

11   **... no, 1793 when the cotton gin was invented ...**

Creative Writing

Cast (2 Female): Rachel, Olivia
Props: Notebooks, pens, textbooks,
various homework materials.

1   *(AT RISE: RACHEL and OLIVIA are sitting at a table doing*
2   *homework.)*
3   **RACHEL:** *(Taps pen on paper, frustrated, then tosses the pen*
4   *away.)* **I'm terrible at creative writing!**
5   **OLIVIA: How can you be terrible at something so easy?**
6   **RACHEL: Two words. Writer's block.**
7   **OLIVIA:** *(Shutting her book)* **I'm finished with my math. Do you**
8   **want me to help you?**
9   **RACHEL: Please!**
10   **OLIVIA: OK, what's your subject?**
11   **RACHEL: Well, we're doing this thing called Creative Writing**
12   **Prompts.**
13   **OLIVIA: What's that?**
14   **RACHEL: It's where you're given a prompt and you're**
15   **supposed to write a story about it.**
16   **OLIVIA: OK. So, what's the prompt?**
17   **RACHEL: An empty glass.**
18   **OLIVIA: An empty glass? That's it?**
19   **RACHEL: That's it. Like I said, I have writer's block. So, there's**
20   **an empty glass. Big deal.**
21   **OLIVIA: I thought it'd be something more exciting. Or at least**
22   **... It was a dark and stormy night ...**
23   **RACHEL: We did that one last week.**
24   **OLIVIA: How did you do?**
25   **RACHEL: Let's just say that Mrs. Hicks wasn't pleased with my**
26   **story. It was short. Very, very short.**
27   **OLIVIA: How short?**

1   RACHEL: It was a dark and stormy night ... so I crawled under
2   my covers and went to sleep. The end. That's how short.
3   OLIVIA: That's terrible.
4   RACHEL: That's what Mrs. Hicks said. I'm telling you, Olivia,
5   I'm not a creative person.
6   OLIVIA: Well, you're in luck because I'm good at creative
7   writing. It's always been easy for me. OK, let me think ...
8   An empty glass ... an empty glass ... an empty glass ...
9   RACHEL: An empty glass was on the table because I got thirsty.
10   The end. Too short?
11   OLIVIA: But *why* were you thirsty?
12   RACHEL: Why?
13   OLIVIA: Yes, *why*?
14   RACHEL: Because it's a normal part of life. Our bodies require
15   fluids. We get thirsty, we drink. Not much to say about
16   that.
17   OLIVIA: And you were thirsty *because* ...
18   RACHEL: Because ... *(Shrugs.)* I don't know.
19   OLIVIA: Maybe because you'd been running.
20   RACHEL: OK, there was an empty glass on the table because I
21   ran around the block and I was thirsty. So, I filled it with
22   water and I drank it. Hey, that was a little longer than my
23   last story. What do you think?
24   OLIVIA: I don't think two sentences will impress Mrs. Hicks.
25   RACHEL: I know, I know. OK, an empty glass ... an empty glass ...
26   OLIVIA: *(Dramatically)* I grabbed the empty glass to throw at
27   the intruder!
28   RACHEL: Hey, that sounds good. *(Writing)*
29   OLIVIA: And with the glass clutched tightly in my hand, I
30   warned the man to leave or else ... or else ...
31   RACHEL: *(Laughing)* Or else I'm going to throw this glass at
32   you?! Olivia, that's stupid! Most people would grab a knife,
33   a gun, or at least a sharp object! But a glass? Who'd be
34   afraid of an empty glass?
35   OLIVIA: OK, OK, we'll try something else. An empty glass ...

1 RACHEL: An empty glass ...

2 OLIVIA: *(Dramatically)* The empty glass would be used to catch

3   all my tears!

4 RACHEL: Yeah, I like that. *(Writing)*

5 OLIVIA: Because after my true love had left me at the altar,

6   there was nothing in the world that I wanted to do except

7   cry! And so I cried! For hours and hours I cried ...

8 RACHEL: *(Suddenly laughing)* And as I cried, I held the empty

9   glass to my eyeball to catch the tears. Olivia, that's stupid!

10   What's she going to do? Drink them? Save them? Freeze

11   them? Water her plants with them?

12 OLIVIA: OK, we'll try something else.

13 RACHEL: I'm not saying your ideas or bad, but it's hard to be

14   creative with an empty glass.

15 OLIVIA: OK, let's keep trying.

16 RACHEL: I have to keep trying if I want to pass the creative

17   writing section in English. OK, an empty glass ... an empty

18   glass ...

19 OLIVIA: *(Suddenly)* I dropped my coins into the empty glass!

20 RACHEL: Why?

21 OLIVIA: *(Dramatically)* Because today, yes, today ... I would

22   begin to save every penny to buy a dress!

23 RACHEL: But I don't wear dresses.

24 OLIVIA: To buy a pair of shoes!

25 RACHEL: *(Laughing)* Why would I want to save my pennies to

26   buy shoes?

27 OLIVIA: Because you're poor and you need some shoes!

28 RACHEL: Well, if I'm poor, maybe I need to save my money for

29   food.

30 OLIVIA: OK, you save your pennies for food!

31 RACHEL: Or I could go to the Salvation Army and get some

32   free food. Then I could save my pennies for something

33   else. Like a new computer!

34 OLIVIA: Do you know how long that would take?

35 RACHEL: *(Laughing)* Yeah. And one empty glass wouldn't even

1   cover the taxes for a new computer.

2 OLIVIA: OK, OK, OK! Let's try something else!

3 RACHEL: *(Wads up several pieces of paper.)* **OK, an empty**

4   **glass ...**

5 OLIVIA: An empty glass ...

6 RACHEL: An empty glass ...

7 OLIVIA: An empty glass ...

8 RACHEL: An empty glass ...

9 OLIVIA: Was all I had left after the fire destroyed my home!

10   The empty glass would be the only keepsake of a life

11   destroyed! And that, I would cherish forever! *(RACHEL*

12   *begins laughing.)* I don't think it's funny!

13 RACHEL: *(Laughing)* Yes, it is! My house burned to the ground,

14   but yea, I have this empty glass to cherish?! That's stupid!

15 OLIVIA: No wonder you are so bad at this creative writing! You

16   don't have a creative bone in your body!

17 RACHEL: I told you I didn't.

18 OLIVIA: Well, good luck. *(Picks up her book as if to leave.)*

19 RACHEL: Wait! Aren't you going to help me?

20 OLIVIA: Why should I? You've made fun of every idea I've had.

21 RACHEL: Olivia, I'm sorry. Can't we just try this just one more

22   time?

23 OLIVIA: We?

24 RACHEL: Olivia, please! I really need your help.

25 OLIVIA: All right, all right. OK, an empty glass ...

26 RACHEL: An empty glass ... *(Not sure about this)* **Dropped on**

27   **the floor and shattered into a million pieces.**

28 OLIVIA: Hey, that's good.

29 RACHEL: The end.

30 OLIVIA: No, keep going, keep going. Then what happened?

31 RACHEL: Then ... then my mother screamed at me for

32   breaking the glass.

33 OLIVIA: OK, keep going.

34 RACHEL: So I blamed it on the cat that always jumped on the

35   kitchen counter.

1   OLIVIA: Keep going.

2   RACHEL: But when my mother noticed the cat asleep on the
3   sofa, she called me a big fat liar!

4   OLIVIA: I don't think your mother would call you a big fat liar.

5   RACHEL: Hey, I'm being creative. And then ... and then my
6   mother came into the kitchen and hit me across the head
7   with the broom!

8   OLIVIA: Whoa! I don't think so.

9   RACHEL: I screamed, "Mother, no! Don't hit me!" But she did
10   it again and again and again!

11   OLIVIA: Rachel, this is a bit violent, don't you think?

12   RACHEL: And blood was streaming down my face! "Forget
13   sweeping the glass," she screamed. "You can pick it up
14   with your bare hands!" So I knelt down on the floor and
15   the glass cut into my flesh. And crying, my hands shook in
16   pain as I picked up the pieces of glass. The end. *(Smiles.)*
17   How was that? Good, huh?

18   OLIVIA: Rachel, I don't know ...

19   RACHEL: Well, I guess I am creative! Who would've thought?

20   OLIVIA: Yeah, but if you could just leave out the part about
21   your mother beating you, that would be good.

22   RACHEL: No, no, that was the best part! And I think I'll add
23   some more about that. *(Writing)* She whacked me on the
24   head over and over as my bloody fingers picked up the
25   sharp pieces of glass ... *(Looks up.)* You know, I like writing.
26   *(OLIVIA shakes her head.)*

Miss Jealous

Cast (1 Male, 1 Female): Zach, Anna

1 ZACH: *(Chasing after ANNA)* **Anna, would you please stop!**
2 ANNA: **Why?**
3 ZACH: **Can't we talk about this?**
4 ANNA: **Oh, now you want to talk? Good! Because I have a**
5 **few things to say to you, *Mr. Don't Blame Me*!**
6 ZACH: **Look, it wasn't my fault!**
7 ANNA: **No?**
8 ZACH: **No!**
9 ANNA: **Oh, please!**
10 ZACH: **Really!**
11 ANNA: **You know what? I don't believe you! So you just go**
12 **ahead and pretend that there's nothing going on**
13 **between you and *Miss Let Me Hang All Over You*! And**
14 **you know what? It's not like you were trying to pry her**
15 **slimy hands off of you!**
16 ZACH: **I tried!**
17 ANNA: **You tried?! You tried?! Well, *Mr. I Tried* ... you didn't**
18 **try hard enough!**
19 ZACH: **Anna, it was her, not me!**
20 ANNA: **Oh, sure! *Mr. Innocent Here*! And what did you do?**
21 **Huh? What did you do?**
22 ZACH: **Nothing!**
23 ANNA: **That's right! Nothing!**
24 ZACH: **Look, don't blame me.**
25 ANNA: **Oh, here we go again, *Mr. Don't Blame Me*! So, if**
26 **Brian Richards put his arms around me, would that**
27 **work with me? Sorry! Don't blame me!**
28 ZACH: **No, I'd take him down!**
29 ANNA: **Is that what I should've done with *Miss Flirty Pants*?**

1   Take her down?

2 ZACH: *(Smiles.)* Hmmm ... That would've been interesting

3   to watch.

4 ANNA: So what were you trying to do? Make me jealous?

5 ZACH: *(Smiles.)* Were you jealous?

6 ANNA: Is that what you were trying to do? Make me jealous?

7 ZACH: No! Like I said, she was the one flirting with me.

8 ANNA: Well, did you ever think that maybe you should

9   remind *Miss Touchy Touchy* that you had a girlfriend?

10 ZACH: I did.

11 ANNA: And?

12 ZACH: *(Chuckles.)* She said she'd like to steal me away from

13   you.

14 ANNA: Oh, isn't that funny! So, is that what you want? For

15   *Miss Boyfriend Stealer* to steal you away?

16 ZACH: No.

17 ANNA: Well, you sure did seem to enjoy it, *Mr. All Smiles*!

18 ZACH: Look, I didn't want to be rude.

19 ANNA: Well, look here, *Mr. Nice Guy*, here's a hint ... The

20   next time some girl puts her hands all over you, push

21   her away!

22 ZACH: *(Smiles.)* Unless it's you, right?

23 ANNA: *(Crosses arms.)* If you're lucky!

24 ZACH: So, are we through fighting?

25 ANNA: Just tell me the truth.

26 ZACH: What?

27 ANNA: Did you like her putting her hands all over you?

28 ZACH: The truth?

29 ANNA: The truth!

30 ZACH: Will you get mad?

31 ANNA: Not if you tell me the truth!

32 ZACH: Well, the truth is ...

33 ANNA: *(Slaps his arm.)* The truth is you did like it, didn't you?

34 ZACH: I thought you weren't going to get mad.

35 ANNA: What do you expect, *Mr. Truthful*? That I'd be happy

1   that my boyfriend of seven months, three weeks, and two
2   days enjoyed having another girl put her hands all over
3   him? *(Pantomimes what the girl had done. He smiles as she*
4   *does this.)* Oh, you're so strong! Do you work out? I love
5   your muscles! Wow! I'm impressed! *(Suddenly, she slaps*
6   *him.)* Stop smiling!
7 ZACH: Wow. Why don't you ever act like that around me?
8 ANNA: Because I don't have to act like that! I'm your
9   girlfriend! Seven months, three weeks, and two days!
10 ZACH: Well, you don't have to get so mad!
11 ANNA: Well, you don't have to be so happy!
12 ZACH: Who's happy?
13 ANNA: You are! And oh, that makes me mad!
14 ZACH: You're mad that I'm happy?
15 ANNA: I'm mad that you're happy when I'm mad because she
16   was so happy to be with you and you were happy to have
17   all the attention and that makes me so mad!
18 ZACH: What?
19 ANNA: Zach, I think we should break up.
20 ZACH: What?!
21 ANNA: I don't want to be with someone who can't be trusted.
22 ZACH: But I didn't do anything!
23 ANNA: No? Well you sure were happy about it ... *Mr. Happy*!
24 ZACH: You're breaking up with me because I'm happy?
25 ANNA: Because you were happy with her!
26 ZACH: I'm not happy with her, I'm happy with you!
27 ANNA: You are?
28 ZACH: Of course I am! I love you!
29 ANNA: *(Puts her arms around him.)* Oh, Zach ...
30 ZACH: Come on, let's go get something to eat ... *Miss Jealous.*

Plays for Three Actors

The Funeral

Cast (3 Female): Denise, Emma, Susan

Prop: A shoebox.

1   DENISE: Well, that was a lovely funeral.

2   EMMA: Funerals aren't lovely.

3   DENISE: I meant it was nice.

4   EMMA: Nice? This was the worst day of my life!

5   SUSAN: You know, you could replace him.

6   EMMA: Replace Fluffy?

7   SUSAN: Not immediately, but when the time is right.

8   EMMA: Susan, no hamster could ever replace Fluffy!

9   SUSAN: But isn't there enough love in your heart for another
10   hamster?

11   EMMA: No! For two years I grew to love Fluffy more than I
12   would've ever imagined. I mean, I told Fluffy everything.
13   All my problems, my hopes, my dreams ... Fluffy was the
14   one person in my life ...

15   DENISE: Uh, Emma ... Fluffy wasn't exactly a person.

16   EMMA: Fluffy was the one *hamster* in my life who truly
17   understood me!

18   SUSAN: *(Stifling a laugh)* I don't mean to laugh, but did you just
19   hear yourself?

20   DENISE: She's upset. Tomorrow will be a better day.

21   EMMA: "Tomorrow will be a better day"? Are you serious? Do
22   you know how hard it's going to be to wake up and look
23   inside Fluffy's little cage and remember all over again
24   that Fluffy is *dead*?!

25   SUSAN: That's why I'm saying that you should replace him.

26   EMMA: And I'm telling you, Fluffy is not replaceable!

27   DENISE: Susan, maybe we should talk about this later.

28   EMMA: Do you know what I remember the most about him?

1   DENISE: What?

2   EMMA: *(Demonstrates.)* All those times I held Fluffy in the palm
3   of my hand, lifted him to my face, and he would lick the tip
4   of my nose. It was so sweet. Oh, Fluffy, I miss you so much!
5   My precious, precious Fluffy!

6   DENISE: Well, at least you won't have to clean his cage anymore.

7   EMMA: That was a mean thing to say!

8   DENISE: I was just trying to find something positive in the
9   situation.

10 SUSAN: And you gave Fluffy the best life ever. You provided him
11   with food, fresh water, a clean cage with lots of toys, and
12   most importantly ... love!

13 EMMA: *(Drops to her knees.)* Oh, Fluffy! Oh, Fluffy, I miss you!
14   *(She hits her hands on the ground.)* How can I go on without
15   you? *(Wailing)* Oh, Fluffy!

16 DENISE: Maybe this isn't a good time to give her our present.

17 SUSAN: No, I don't think so, either. Look at her!

18 DENISE: Well, we've got to do something!

19 SUSAN: OK. *(Picks up nearby shoebox.)* Emma, we got you
20   something. *(EMMA looks up.)* It's a present. We hope you like
21   it.

22 EMMA: A present for me?

23 SUSAN: We thought this would help you feel better.

24 EMMA: *(Sits up, wipes her tears, and takes the box.)* Thank you.
25   What is it? A miniature headstone? Did you have it engraved
26   for Fluffy?

27 DENISE: Just open it and look.

28 EMMA: *(Opens the box, screams, then shuts it quickly.)* I don't
29   want this!

30 DENISE: We're just trying to help.

31 EMMA: Take this away!

32 SUSAN: But we can't take it back. The pet store doesn't take
33   returns. It's some new policy they have. No returns.

34 DENISE: Then what are we going to do with it? My mom won't let
35   me keep it.

1   SUSAN: Neither will mine. I guess we can let it go. Maybe, just
2   maybe, it can take care of itself.
3   DENISE: But won't one of the neighborhood cats get it?
4   SUSAN: Probably. But there's nothing else to do since Emma
5   doesn't want it. *(Kneels down and opens the box.)* Go on, little
6   hamster. Go on. You can do it. You can survive in the
7   wilderness.
8   EMMA: *(Grabs the box.)* Give that to me! This little baby hamster
9   won't last one day out there!
10 SUSAN: But what else can we do?
11 DENISE: I know. Maybe if you give us your cage, we can find
12   someone who'll take it.
13 EMMA: I'm not giving away Fluffy's cage!
14 DENISE: It was just an idea.
15 SUSAN: Well, it can just live in this uncomfortable shoebox until
16   we find it a new home. Emma, do you think I could borrow
17   some food so the baby doesn't get hungry?
18 DENISE: *(Looking inside the box)* Poor thing. It does look hungry.
19 SUSAN: Probably starving. I don't think they treat the hamsters
20   very well at that pet store. Poor little thing.
21 DENISE: I wonder if it's a boy or a girl? It's cute. Can I hold him?
22   Or her?
23 EMMA: No, too many strange hands are not good for a hamster. I
24   think it's a boy like Fluffy. Oh, he does look hungry. Are you
25   hungry, little guy? You are? Well, let's go get you something
26   to eat. And how about a soft little bed, too? I have this cage
27   that you would love. It's even got a little wheel for you to play
28   on. Yes, Yes, I know. Mama's going to take care of the baby.
29   *(She exits.)*
30 DENISE: *"Mama"?*
31 SUSAN: Well, it worked. *(They high five.)* She completely forgot
32   about Fluffy.
33 DENISE: Well, let's just hope this one lives for a long, long time!

Teacher's Aide

Cast (1 Male, 2 Female): Mrs. Cox, Paul, Wendy
Props: A stack of papers, two red pens.
Setting: A classroom.

1 MRS. COX: Paul, thank you for agreeing to be my teacher's aide
2   this semester.

3 PAUL: You're welcome.

4 MRS. COX: This class is my conference period, so there won't
5   be any students in here unless they're here for tutoring or
6   make-up work. And since I don't have anything scheduled
7   for today, I'll be in the teacher's lounge.

8 PAUL: You're leaving?

9 MRS. COX: I'll be back before the bell rings.

10 PAUL: But what do you want me to do?

11 MRS. COX: Uh ... *(Looking around her desk)* Here. Grade these
12   papers.

13 PAUL: Me?

14 MRS. COX: Sure, why not? Let me tell you, I am sick to death of
15   reading essays about "My Favorite Childhood Memory."
16   Look Paul, all you have to do is read the paper, then maybe
17   add a few comments such as, "Interesting!" "Great!" "I
18   liked this story a lot!" Or you can make suggestions such
19   as, "Try to be more descriptive." Or, "What did you mean
20   by this?" Anyway, just grade them however you want. I
21   don't care.

22 PAUL: But ...

23 MRS. COX: And don't worry about the spelling. This is a
24   creative writing class, and we don't get hung up about
25   spelling.

26 PAUL: But ...

27 MRS. COX: I know, I know, it's boring, but you did sign up to be

1   my teacher's aide.
2   PAUL: But I thought I'd be going to the office and making copies
3   or stapling papers or things like that. I didn't know I'd be
4   grading papers!
5   MRS. COX: Look Paul, I have over a hundred and fifty students,
6   and I don't have time to read all their stupid stories. I can
7   give out the assignments, help with ideas, give examples,
8   but read them all? Well, that's what you're for.
9   WENDY: *(Enters.)* Mrs. Cox, can I sit in here during the rest of my
10   lunch period and work on my story for your class?
11 MRS. COX: Absolutely! And Paul will be in here, too. He's my new
12   teacher's aide. Now, I'm off to the lounge for a stiff drink. I
13   mean ... large Coke! Have fun! *(Exits.)*
14 WENDY: *(Sits down beside PAUL.)* What are you working on?
15 PAUL: Mrs. Cox expects me to grade all these papers!
16 WENDY: What? Are you serious?
17 PAUL: Yeah! She expects me to read them and grade them for her.
18   Can you believe that? I've never even taken a creative
19   writing class. Heck, I'm barely making a C in English!
20 WENDY: That's weird.
21 PAUL: Mrs. Cox said she doesn't like to read her students'
22   assignments, so that's what I'm here to do.
23 WENDY: Wow. That means you'll be grading my paper.
24 PAUL: Heck, I'll give everyone an A! *(Mimics writing.)* Good job! A!
25   Wonderful! A! Excellent! A! Everyone gets an A!
26 WENDY: Wow, this is great! And since you're going to give me an
27   A, I can just sit here and relax and not stress out over my
28   paper. Hey, I know! Why don't you go ahead and put an A on
29   the top of my paper.
30 PAUL: But you haven't even written it yet.
31 WENDY: I know, but I will.
32 PAUL: *(Shrugs.)* OK, why not? *(Puts an A on her paper.)*
33 WENDY: Thanks! I wish you were the teacher's aide in all my
34   classes!
35 PAUL: Well, I'm glad I'm not!

1   **WENDY:** Hey, you want me to help you grade those papers?

2   **PAUL:** Yeah, thanks! *(Gives her half the stack of papers.)* **And**

3   **here's a red pen for you to grade with.**

4   **WENDY:** Thank you very much. *(Looking at the first paper)*

5   **Ooooh! I can't stand Reid Johnson! He is so obnoxious and**

6   **rude! And look what he wrote! "My favorite childhood**

7   **memory is when I painted green stripes in my sister's hair**

8   **while she was asleep." Oh! He's so mean! I want to give**

9   **him a big fat F!**

10 **PAUL:** Go ahead. I don't care.

11 **WENDY:** Are you serious?

12 **PAUL:** Why not? Mrs. Cox said I could grade them however I

13   wanted. So, be my guest!

14 **WENDY:** *(Smiling)* **Thanks!** *(Writes a huge F on the paper.)* **That**

15   **felt good!**

16 **PAUL:** And look at this one. *(Talking in a baby tone)* **"My**

17   **Favorite Childhood Memory, by Ashley Brown. I was just**

18   **three months old when I was crowned Beautiful Baby."**

19   **Like she could remember being three months old! "And**

20   **ever since that day, I have been told that I was beautiful. I**

21   **know it's not a talent, but that day, when I was three**

22   **months old, was the beginning of my career as a beautiful**

23   **person."**

24 **WENDY:** Oh, she's such a snob!

25 **PAUL:** Hmmm ... what should I give her? I know! How about an

26   F for being so ugly and conceited! *(Writes a large F on her*

27   *paper.)*

28 **WENDY:** Oh, and look at this one! Joe Porter says, "My favorite

29   memory was squishing centipedes in the street with my

30   best friend, Billy." Gross! *(Marks a big F on his paper.)*

31 **PAUL:** Oh, and I can't stand this guy! He's getting a big fat F!

32   *(Puts an F on the paper.)*

33 **WENDY:** And this girl rubbed mud on my gym clothes last

34   year. F!

35 **PAUL:** And here's Mr. Big Man on campus!

1   WENDY: Who, Brad? *(Takes the paper from him.)* **Let me see**
2   **that.** *(Dreamy)* **Oh, he should get an A!**
3   PAUL: *(Takes the paper back.)* **I don't think so! This guy tripped**
4   **me in the hall a couple of weeks ago. Oh yeah, everyone**
5   **thought it was funny, but I didn't! So, an F for Mr. Brad!**
6   WENDY: **You know, I like grading papers. This is fun.**
7   PAUL: **Yeah, it's not as hard as I thought it was going to be.**
8   WENDY: **Hey, if you ever need me to help again, just let me**
9   **know.**
10 PAUL: **Yeah, thanks.**
11 WENDY: **And thank you for my A!**
12 PAUL: **You're welcome.**
13 WENDY: **And you know, since you'll be grading all the papers**
14   **this year, do you think, well, I hate to ask, but ...**
15 PAUL: **Hey, don't worry about it. You're going to make straight**
16   **A's in this class!**
17 WENDY: *(Hugs him.)* **Oh, thank you!**
18 MRS. COX: *(Enters.)* **So, how's it going?**
19 PAUL: **Uh, great.**
20 MRS. COX: *(Looking at the graded papers.)* **F, F, F, F, F, F ... Paul,**
21   **would you mind explaining this?**
22 PAUL: **Uh ...**
23 WENDY: *(Jumps up.)* **Blame me, Mrs. Cox! I was helping Paul,**
24   **and I'm the one who put most of those F's on the papers.**
25 MRS. COX: **Most of the F's? They're *all* F's!** *(Picking up a paper)*
26   **Except for yours, Miss Reaves! You got an A, and you**
27   **haven't even written the paper! That's a new one for me!**
28 PAUL: *(Stands.)* **Don't blame her, Mrs. Cox. It was me.**
29 MRS. COX: **And do you care to explain to me *why* you put F's on**
30   **all of these papers?**
31 PAUL: **Uh ... they weren't very good?**
32 MRS. COX: **Well, Mr. Teacher's Aide, I'd like you to write an**
33   **essay on why being cruel to your classmates isn't very**
34   **nice. *And* I would like you to be here to read it out loud to**
35   **all of my classes!**

1   PAUL: Oh, I couldn't do that! I mean, read it out loud! I have
2   stage fright, Mrs. Cox!
3   MRS. COX: All right, then we'll let the students vote on your
4   grade. Sight unseen! And Miss Reaves, I think an A is way
5   too high for this paper ... this paper that hasn't even been
6   written!
7   WENDY: But I was going to ...
8   MRS. COX: *(Writes on paper.)* Not an A, but an F!
9   WENDY: But ...
10   PAUL: Does this mean you don't want me to grade your papers
11   anymore?
12   MRS. COX: Are you kidding? I'm not grading all those papers!
13   But you're going to learn to give everyone an A! A for
14   effort! Got it?
15   PAUL: Yes, ma'am!
16   WENDY: But I didn't get an A for effort.
17   MRS. COX: Well, maybe if you actually write your paper, you
18   will!
19   WENDY: *(Smiles.)* Thank you, Mrs. Cox.
20   MRS. COX: All right, I'm going back to the lounge for another
21   drink. You know, another Coke. Wendy, you get started on
22   that paper. And Paul, get the White Out and change those
23   F's to A's.
24   PAUL and WENDY: Yes, ma'am!

Plays for
Four Actors

Happy Birthday

Cast (1 Male, 3 Female): Courtney, Libby, Peter, Brenda
Prop: CD wrapped in birthday paper.
Setting: Outside a classroom.

1   *(AT RISE: COURTNEY and LIBBY begin singing "Happy*
2   *Birthday" to PETER as he enters.)*
3   **COURTNEY and LIBBY:** Happy birthday to you, happy
4   birthday to you, happy birthday dear Peter, happy
5   birthday to you!
6   **PETER:** Uh ... what was that for?
7   **COURTNEY:** It's your birthday, silly!
8   **LIBBY:** Happy birthday!
9   **PETER:** Oh, well, thanks.
10   **COURNTEY:** We wanted to buy you a present ...
11   **LIBBY:** But we were broke! Sorry!
12   **PETER:** That's uh ... OK. But thanks, anyway. *(Starts to walk*
13   *away.)*
14   **LIBBY:** So, are we the first two people to sing "Happy
15   Birthday" to you?
16   **PETER:** The first two.
17   **COURTNEY:** *(Singing)* Happy birthday to you, happy birthday
18   to you, happy birthday dear Peter, happy birthday to you!
19   **PETER:** OK. Well, thanks again.
20   **LIBBY:** I wish they'd hurry and open the door. I hate zero hour,
21   don't you?
22   **PETER:** Uh, yeah.
23   **COURTNEY:** Not me because I'm a morning person! And I
24   always have so much more energy in the mornings! That's
25   why I take zero hour. Not that Biology is that much fun,
26   but at least I'm happier about it in the mornings.
27   **PETER:** I hate mornings.

1 LIBBY: Me too.

2 COURTNEY: Well, not today, because today is your birthday!

3   *(Singing)* Happy birthday to you, happy birthday to you,

4   happy birthday dear Peter, happy birthday to you!

5 PETER: *(Giving her a strange look)* And thanks again. By the

6   way, how did you know it was my birthday?

7 COURTNEY: Well, I work in the school office and I saw your

8   file.

9 PETER: You were snooping through my file?

10 COURTNEY: Not snooping, just looking. Updating, actually.

11   And I couldn't help but notice that today was your

12   birthday. One day after mine.

13 PETER: So yesterday was your birthday?

14 COURTNEY: Yes.

15 PETER: Oh.

16 LIBBY: Well, aren't you going to wish Libby a happy birthday?

17 PETER: Her birthday was yesterday.

18 LIBBY: Well, you could say "Happy belated birthday."

19 PETER: Yeah, whatever.

20 BRENDA: *(Enters, carrying a gift, runs to PETER and gives him a*

21   *hug.)* Oh Peter, happy birthday!

22 PETER: Thanks, Brenda.

23 BRENDA: *(Offers him the gift.)* Here. I hope you like it.

24 PETER: Thanks!

25 BRENDA: It's that CD you wanted!

26 PETERS: Thanks, Brenda!

27 COURTNEY: We already sang "Happy Birthday" to him.

28 LIBBY: Want us to sing it again?

29 PETER: No! Please, no.

30 BRENDA: *(Pulls PETER aside.)* Who are those girls?

31 PETER: Beats me. I've never seen them in my life! They claim

32   to be in my zero hour class, but I don't know ...

33 BRENDA: You don't recognize them?

34 PETER: No.

35 BRENDA: That's strange.

1   PETER: Hey, maybe it's a joke. You know, maybe there's a
2   hidden camera over there, and they're all just waiting to
3   jump out and surprise me!
4   BRENDA: A hidden camera? Peter, I don't think so.
5   PETER: *(Looking around in the distance)* No, I saw something
6   like this on TV awhile back.
7   BRENDA: And you're sure you don't know those girls?
8   PETER: Positive. *(Spots something.)* Hey, I think that's it!
9   BRENDA: What?
10   PETER: *(Pointing)* The camera! See?
11   BRENDA: No, not really.
12   PETER: I knew it! Hey, you better smile; you're gonna to be on
13   TV with me!
14   BRENDA: *(Gives a fake smile.)* But I don't see the camera.
15   PETER: So listen, we need to act surprised by whatever
16   happens. OK?
17   BRENDA: *(Smiling)* OK. But what do you think is going to
18   happen?
19   PETER: I don't know, but I bet it'll be good.
20   BRENDA: *(Still smiling)* Are you sure that's a camera?
21   PETER: *(To the other girls)* Hey look, if you want to sing "Happy
22   Birthday" to me again, go right ahead.
23   LIBBY: Great! I'm glad to see you're finally getting into the
24   birthday spirit!
25   COURTNEY: OK, here we go!
26   COURTNEY, LIBBY, and BRENDA: *(Singing)* Happy birthday to
27   you, happy birthday to you, happy birthday dear Peter,
28   happy birthday to you!
29   PETER: That was great! Thank you! Thank you so much! *(Gives
30   COURTNEY and LIBBY a hug.)* OK, what's next?
31   LIBBY: Sorry we don't have a gift for you.
32   PETER: Oh, come on. I know you have something for me. A
33   little surprise!
34   COURTNEY: *(Suddenly)* Oh, OK! *(Kisses his cheek.)*
35   LIBBY: Oh, yeah! *(Kisses his other cheek.)*

1   PETER: That's it?

2   LIBBY: I think so.

3   COURTNEY: Sorry, but we're broke.

4   PETER: Oh, you're not fooling me. I know you can do better

5   than that. *(Smiles toward the camera.)*

6   LIBBY: Oh, OK! *(Suddenly kisses him on the mouth.)* How was

7   that?

8   PETER: *(Spitting and wiping his mouth)* Why did you do *that*?

9   LIBBY: I thought you wanted me to!

10 PETER: No! Yuck!

11 BRENDA: I think you can forget about the camera. And look, I

12   think it just flew away.

13 COURTNEY: What camera?

14 BRENDA: Oh, just something he was hoping to get for his

15   birthday.

16 COURTNEY: Sorry we didn't get you a camera, but we're broke.

17   But we can sing "Happy Birthday" to you again!

18 LIBBY: Good idea, Courtney!

19 COURTNEY and LIBBY: *(Singing)* Happy birthday to you,

20   happy birthday to you, happy birthday dear Peter, happy

21   birthday to you!

22 PETER: *(As they are singing)* Stop! Please, just stop!

23 COURTNEY: Don't you like it?

24 PETER: Look, I'm sorry, but I don't even know you!

25 BRENDA: That makes two of us.

26 PETER: You claim to be in my zero hour class, but I've never

27   seen you in my life!

28 COURTNEY: That's crazy.

29 LIBBY: But we sit right next to you.

30 PETER: Then I guess I need some glasses because I've never

31   seen either one of you in my entire life!

32 LIBBY: But how can that be? Yesterday you asked to borrow my

33   highlighter.

34 COURTNEY: And I gave you three answers to that review page.

35 PETER: What answers, what review page, what highlighter?

1   Am I losing my mind?

2 BRENDA: Are you two playing some sort of trick on Peter?

3   Because if you are, I'm going to talk to the principal about it!

4 LIBBY: It's no trick.

5 COURTNEY: We were just trying to be nice by singing "Happy

6   Birthday."

7 LIBBY: Yeah. *(COURTNEY and LIBBY exchange looks and begin*

8   *singing "Happy Birthday" again.)*

9 PETER: Stop it! Stop it! Will you please just stop it? *(Pause)* **What's**

10   **really going on here?** *(Pointing at COURTNEY and LIBBY)* **I**

11   **don't know you! And I don't know you!** *(Points to LIBBY.)* **And**

12   ***you*, you even kissed me on the lips!**

13 LIBBY: Did you like it?

14 PETER: Yes! I mean, *no*! I mean ... I'm so confused! *(Points finger*

15   *in LIBBY's face.)* **Are you sure there's no hidden camera?**

16 LIBBY: What hidden camera?

17 COURTNEY: I'm sorry we didn't buy you a camera, but we told

18   you ... we're broke!

19 LIBBY: And we're sorry, OK? We didn't even know you wanted a

20   camera!

21 BRENDA: OK, OK, this is enough.

22 PETER: Brenda, you know, maybe you should take me to the

23   hospital for some tests. I think something is wrong with me.

24 BRENDA: Nothing is wrong with you. But something is wrong

25   with them. *(To COURTNEY and LIBBY)* **OK, who put you up**

26   **to this? I want to know this very second!**

27 COURTNEY: Put us up to what?

28 LIBBY: We were just trying to be nice by singing "Happy

29   Birthday" to him. *(COURTNEY and LIBBY exchange looks and*

30   *begin singing.)*

31 BRENDA: Stop it! Stop it! *Stop it!* *(They stop.)* **Why are you doing**

32   **this to him?**

33 LIBBY: We were trying to be nice! Haven't you ever wanted to

34   sing "Happy Birthday" to a friend before?

35 PETER: But we're not friends! At least ... at least I don't think

1   we're friends. Brenda, you're my friend, aren't you?

2   BRENDA: Of course I'm your friend, Peter. Why are you asking

3   me that?

4   PETER: I was just checking. I just don't get this. I really asked to

5   borrow your highlighter?

6   LIBBY: It was pink. My pink highlighter.

7   PETER: And you gave me some answers for that review?

8   COURTNEY: You thanked me at least twice for helping you.

9   PETER: And we all sit by each other?

10   COURTNEY: And sometimes we pass notes. Remember?

11   PETER: No. No, I don't remember!

12   LIBBY: And you're always talking about Brenda.

13   BRENDA: He is? And what does he say about me?

14   LIBBY: Oh, that he likes you and loves playing jokes on you and

15   that you'll never be able to get him back because he never

16   falls for jokes the way you do.

17   BRENDA: *(Smiles.)* Isn't that interesting. Why, Peter would never

18   fall for a joke, huh? *(The girls giggle.)*

19   PETER: *(After a pause)* You mean ... you mean *you* put them up to

20   this?

21   BRENDA: I owed you one. Actually I owed you more than one so

22   I thought I'd make it good! Oh! I got you good, didn't I?

23   PETER: This is not funny, Brenda!

24   BRENDA: Do you still want a ride to the hospital?

25   PETER: It's not funny, Brenda!

26   BRENDA: And too bad that camera over there had to fly away. I

27   couldn't have even thought of that myself! *(The girls laugh.)*

28   PETER: I knew it! I knew I hadn't seen you two before!

29   COURTNEY: You're right. We don't even go to this school.

30   LIBBY: So, you probably won't be seeing us again. So, before we

31   leave, let us at least wish you a happy birthday! *(COURTNEY*

32   *and LIBBY exchange looks, then begin singing "Happy*

33   *Birthday." BRENDA joins them as PETER can't help but smile*

34   *and shake his head.)*

The Kissing Booth

Cast (2 Male, 2 Female): Alex, Ken, Stacy, Carla
Props: Poster board, two stuffed animals (dog and cat), two $5 bills.

1   *(AT RISE: STACY and CARLA are sitting at a table. A poster*
2   *board hangs from the table which reads: "KISSES: $5.00."*
3   *ALEX and KEN enter.)*
4   **ALEX:** *(Holds out five dollars.)* **Do I get to choose who gives me**
5   **the kiss?**
6   **STACY: Certainly.**
7   **ALEX: Decisions, decisions.**
8   **CARLA:** *(Takes the money.)* **And we do appreciate you**
9   **supporting our club.**
10   **KEN: What club is that?**
11   **CARLA: The Matchmaker Club.**
12   **KEN: What's that about?**
13   **ALEX: I know. It's a club whose main objective is to help**
14   **people find true love, right?**
15   **CARLA: I'm sorry, but that's wrong.**
16   **KEN: Good guess, though.**
17   **ALEX: OK, then what are you matching up?**
18   **STACY: Animals.**
19   **KEN: Animals? Don't they kinda sniff at each other, and then**
20   **maybe wag their tails or growl to see if they like each**
21   **other? I mean, whoever thought of a matchmaking**
22   **service for animals. I'm sorry, but that sounds really**
23   **stupid.**
24   **ALEX: People actually pay for this?**
25   **STACY: It's a free service.**
26   **KEN:** *(Laughing)* **I can see it now!** *(Takes Stacy's hand.)* **Yes, we**
27   **are here to offer you, I mean, offer your dog the chance to**

1   find true love. We've electronically matched little Fifi here
2   with Butch. And won't they make fine puppies!
3   STACY: *(Takes her hand away.)* You are so stupid.
4   KEN: Well, your club sounds pretty stupid!
5   ALEX: Hey, look! There's a dog. Want me to bring it over and let
6   you do your matchmaking?
7   CARLA: We are not helping animals find true love, you idiot!
8   ALEX: Then what are you doing?
9   CARLA: Matching up stray, neglected, and lost dogs with potential
10   owners.
11   ALEX and KEN: Oh!
12   STACY: People come to us who want to adopt a pet.
13   ALEX and KEN: Oh!
14   CARLA: So, are you ready for your kisses?
15   ALEX: Kisses? I get more than one?
16   CARLA: As many as you want.
17   KEN: *(Takes out a five dollar bill.)* I'll take some kisses, too!
18   STACY: *(Takes his money.)* Thank you. It's for a good cause.
19   KEN: Helping pets get adopted. Yeah, that's a good cause. OK, let's
20   see ... which girl do I choose?
21   ALEX: Decisions, decisions.
22   KEN: You are both pretty cute. And both available? I mean, no
23   serious boyfriends?
24   CARLA: I'm sorry, but we are both dedicated to our cause.
25   KEN: Dedication is fine, but you still have to have a social life.
26   STACY: Our social life consists of finding homes for the
27   homeless.
28   ALEX: You mean stray animals?
29   STACY: Yes.
30   ALEX: And it is a worthy cause, but surely you would like to go
31   out sometime ... like on a date?
32   STACY: There's hardly any time for that.
33   CARLA: Yes, we are two busy, busy girls.
34   ALEX: How about Saturday night? We'll all get together and go
35   see a movie.

1   KEN: Isn't that a great idea? Hey, Alex, could I talk to you for a
2   minute?
3   ALEX: Sure. Excuse us. *(They move to the side.)*
4   KEN: We need to decide who gets who. I like the girl on the
5   right. What about you?
6   ALEX: That's the one I wanted.
7   KEN: OK, OK, then I'll take the girl on the left. But are we
8   talking about our right and left or their right and left?
9   ALEX: Our left.
10 KEN: But that'd mean the girl on the right is the girl I wanted,
11   right?
12 ALEX: I don't know! You're confusing me.
13 KEN: OK, you get the one on the left and I get the one on the
14   right, right?
15 ALEX: Right. At least, I think that's right. *(They go back to the
16   girls. After much confusion and swapping places, they try to
17   stand in front of the girl they had chosen.)*
18 KEN: OK, we'd like our kisses now.
19 STACY: OK. Close your eyes and pucker up. *(The girls turn
20   around and each get a stuffed dog or cat. As they wipe the
21   boys' faces with the stuffed animals, they make cat and dog
22   sounds. The boys open their eyes and jump back.)*
23 ALEX: Hey, what are you doing?
24 KEN: What happened to our kisses?
25 CARLA: Those were animal kisses. Weren't they sweet?
26 STACY: And doesn't that just make you want to adopt a poor
27   homeless puppy or kitty?
28 ALEX and KEN: *No!*
29 CARLA: Where's your compassion?
30 STACY: Don't you love animals?
31 KEN: Yes we love animals, but we thought we were paying for
32   *real* kisses!
33 CARLA: Well, can't we save that for our date?
34 ALEX: You mean ... y'all still want to go out with us?
35 CARLA: Sure we do.

1   **ALEX:** Great, but we still have one little problem.

2   **CARLA and STACY:** What?

3   **KEN:** Yeah, what's that?

4   **ALEX:** We need a matchmaker to figure out who gets who!

5   *(They all laugh.)*

Tryouts

Cast (1 Male, 3 Female): Dawn, Callie, Robin, Leon
Props: Scripts.
Setting: An empty classroom.

1   *(AT RISE: DAWN, CALLIE, and ROBIN enter, each*
2   *carrying a script.)*
3 DAWN: I heard there are eight girls trying out for three
4   parts.
5 CALLIE: Eight?
6 DAWN: At least.
7 ROBIN: Then it's a good thing we decided to stay after
8   school and practice.
9 CALLIE: This is going to be tough.
10 ROBIN: Then let's think positive. We are talented. We are
11   believable. And we are perfect for these roles.
12 CALLIE: Forget the fact that none of us have been in drama
13   until this semester. But OK, I'll think positive.
14 DAWN: Let's get started.
15 ROBIN: I've never even heard of this play.
16 DAWN: It's because Mr. Morgan wrote it himself.
17 ROBIN: He did?
18 DAWN: *(Holding up the script)* See? By J.H. Morgan.
19 CALLIE: Well, too bad he didn't write more parts for girls.
20   And look at their names! Jane, Ida, and Harriet.
21 ROBIN: Those are old names. Why didn't he choose
22   something more contemporary? Like ... Scarlet. Or
23   Alexandra. Or Robina?
24 DAWN and CALLIE: Robina?
25 ROBIN: *(Points to herself.)* Robin, Robina. At least it sounds
26   theatrical.
27 DAWN: Well, Mr. Morgan is old, and he doesn't have a clue

1 what sounds good. Oh well, we better get started. I'll be
2 Jane, Callie can be Ida, and Robin can be Harriet.
3 *(Reading dryly from the script)* **Oh Ida, if he doesn't**
4 **propose, I think I might die. Yes, I shall take a sword**
5 **and plunge it into my chest.**
6 CALLIE: *(Reading dryly)* **Oh, don't speak of such things,**
7 **Jane. Surely you won't die.**
8 DAWN: **Oh, but indeed I will. Death will be my only relief.**
9 ROBIN: *(Also reading dryly)* **But Jane, Edgar doesn't deserve**
10 **your love.**
11 DAWN: **Harriet, how can you speak such nonsense?**
12 ROBIN: **But Jane, Edgar has trampled on so many hearts,**
13 **and yours shall surely be next. You must remain**
14 **strong. Strong like the ox.**
15 CALLIE: **Harriet is right. You must remain strong.**
16 DAWN: **But Edgar has captured my heart. How could I ever**
17 **love another? The truth is I can't. Never will my heart**
18 **belong to another man. I shall spend my entire life**
19 **loving him. Or death, may you come!**
20 ROBIN: **But Edgar has promised his heart to so many, yet**
21 **he does not stay true to his promises.**
22 DAWN: **But perhaps I am the one. Finally his love has met**
23 **the right match.**
24 CALLIE: **And how shall you truly know?**
25 DAWN: **Tonight I shall know.**
26 CALLIE: **Tonight?**
27 DAWN: **Yes, tonight. Edgar has promised to meet me here at**
28 **this very spot with his answer.**
29 ROBIN: **His answer?**
30 DAWN: **His answer regarding his love for me. In fact, he**
31 **should be here any moment now. Yes, any moment now**
32 **and I will know my fate. Love or death!**
33 CALLIE: **But Jane, you mustn't choose death if he turns**
34 **from you. You must remain strong. You must have faith**
35 **that love will show itself again.**

1 DAWN: Oh, but I have faith. I have faith that Edgar will
2   appear and announce his undying love for me!
3 LEON: *(Enters.)* Hey.
4 DAWN: *(Rushes to him and wraps her arms around him.*
5   *Dramatically)* **Oh my love! My dearest love!**
6 LEON: Uh, what's going on?
7 DAWN: Tell me, oh, please tell me that you love me!
8 LEON: Tell you that I love you?
9 DAWN: Yes, so that death does not take me! Please my love;
10   tell me that your heart is mine!
11 LEON: Uh ... OK. Sure. I guess. You know, Dawn, you
12   could've just passed me a note in Biology class telling
13   me you liked me or something. *(CALLIE and ROBIN*
14   *laugh.)*
15 DAWN: But I was so afraid! Had you rejected me ... oh, just
16   the thought!
17 LEON: So, you really like me?
18 DAWN: *(Reading from the script)* **Then it's true?**
19 LEON: What?
20 DAWN: You're proclaiming your everlasting love to me?
21 LEON: I don't know about everlasting, but we could catch a
22   movie this weekend if you want to.
23 DAWN: Marriage? You said marriage?
24 LEON: *Whoa!* I didn't say anything about marriage!
25 DAWN: Oh, my darling, yes of course I'll marry you! Ida,
26   Harriet, did you hear? He asked me to marry him!
27 LEON: No, I didn't!
28 CALLIE: *(Reading from the script)* **Oh, how wonderful!**
29 ROBIN: Yes, we're so happy for you. I will gather every
30   flower in town to bring to the ceremony.
31 CALLIE: And I shall help. It will be the most beautiful
32   ceremony ever!
33 LEON: Hey, look ,Dawn, I'll take you to a movie, but I'm not
34   getting hitched!
35 DAWN: Oh, good-bye death! Good-bye! A sword shall not

1   pierce my heart after all!

2   LEON: So, uh, call me about the movie, OK? And I'll, uh ...
3   see you later, OK?

4   DAWN: Good-bye my love! Until we meet again! *(LEON exits.*
5   *The girls laugh.)*

6   ROBIN: Oh Leon, you have saved our friend from death!

7   CALLIE: Yes, the sword shall not become her!

8   DAWN: So, do you think that was any good?

9   ROBIN: Not until Leon, but after that I thought you were
10   pretty good.

11 DAWN: Well, even though the characters have stupid
12   names, I really want this part!

13 ROBIN: Then try pretending that Edgar is some guy you are
14   crazy about.

15 CALLIE: How about Landon?

16 DAWN: That might work.

17 CALLIE: Pretend I'm Landon and say a few lines.

18 DAWN: OK. *(Reading dryly)* Tell me, oh, please tell me that
19   you love me.

20 ROBIN: I'm sorry, but that was bad.

21 CALLIE: Dawn, you wouldn't talk to Landon like that.

22 DAWN: You're right, Callie! Because I wouldn't have the
23   nerve to talk to him like that. *(Dramatically)* Tell me; oh
24   please tell me that you love me?

25 ROBIN: Hey, that was better! But next time don't make it a
26   question.

27 DAWN: OK, let's try this again. Robin, you stand here and
28   be Landon.

29 ROBIN: OK. *(Deep voice)* Yes, I am Landon.

30 DAWN: *(Dryly)* Oh Edgar, tell me, oh please tell me that you
31   love me.

32 ROBIN: I'm sorry, but that's sounds bad. You've got to put
33   more feeling into it.

34 DAWN: Oh, I'm never going to get this!

35 CALLIE: You did better when Leon was here. Dawn, do

1   you like Leon?

2 DAWN: Of course I like Leon. He's a sweetheart and cute

3   and all that ... but, he's not interested in me.

4 ROBIN: Then why did he ask you out?

5 DAWN: He did?

6 ROBIN: Didn't you hear?

7 DAWN: Well, I wasn't really paying attention. I was having

8   too much fun teasing him. He really asked me out?

9 CALLIE: He sure did. Remember, he thought you wanted to

10   get married, but he was willing to settle for a movie?

11 ROBIN: He is cute.

12 DAWN: Wow. I must've really impressed him with my

13   acting. He really believed that I liked him. I mean I do,

14   but I didn't think he did, so I wasn't trying to act like I

15   liked him only act like I liked him, you know what I

16   mean?

17 ROBIN: I think. Well, anyway, why don't we try this again?

18   Instead of being Landon, I'll be Leon. OK? Ready?

19 DAWN: OK. Let me just gather my thoughts for a minute.

20   *(Walking away, she takes a deep breath and looks at the*

21   *script. She doesn't realize this, but LEON enters. Quickly,*

22   *she turns around to ROBIN.)* **Oh, Leon!**

23 LEON: Yes? *(They are all surprised to see him.)*

24 DAWN: You're here?

25 LEON: Yes. What did you want to say?

26 CALLIE: Don't stop now, Dawn. Remember, you really want

27   this. Take advantage of the moment.

28 LEON: Well?

29 DAWN: Uh, OK. *(Looks at the script, then dramatically)* **Oh,**

30   **Leon, tell me, oh please tell me that you love me!**

31 LEON: Look, I think love is a bit sudden, but I do like you a

32   lot. And who knows, after time, we may fall in love.

33 ROBIN: That was good.

34 CALLIE: Much better.

35 LEON: So, about this weekend. Do you still want to go?

1   DAWN: Yeah, I would! Thanks.

2   CALLIE: Oh, and now death shall not become our friend!

3   LEON: Huh? *(The girls laugh.)*

4   ROBIN: Jane has found true love after all!

5   DAWN: And I really, really want this part!

6   LEON: What part? Are y'all practicing for a play or
7   something?

8   CALLIE: How did you guess?

9   LEON: So that was just a joke? You were just teasing about
10   wanting to go out with me?

11   DAWN: No, I mean, yes. I mean, yes and no. Oh, come on! I'll
12   explain everything to you. *(DAWN and LEON exit.)*

13   ROBIN: *(To Callie)* Oh tell me, please tell me that you love
14   me!

15   CALLIE: *(Ignoring her)* I'm hungry. Let's go get something
16   to eat.

17   ROBIN: But if you don't love me, I shall take a sword and
18   plunge in into my heart!

19   CALLIE: You want to share some nachos at The Shack?

20   ROBIN: But what about our love?

21   CALLIE: Come on, I'm hungry!

22   ROBIN: Oh death, you are to be my only relief from this
23   misery!

24   CALLIE: Fine, I'm going to get something to eat.

25   ROBIN: Please my love; tell me that your heart is mine!

26   CALLIE: Bye! *(Exits.)*

27   ROBIN: *(Running after CALLIE)* Hey, wait up! I'm hungry,
28   too!

Dead Zone

Cast (3 Male, 1 Female): Alan, Michelle, Tyler, Salesman
Props: Cellphone, school supplies, car keys.
Setting: An office supply store.

1   *(AT RISE: ALAN enters talking on his cellphone. He carries a*
2   *few school supplies.)*
3   **ALAN: Mom, this is the sixth time you've called me! I know, I**
4   **know, but ... Mom, listen, I ... OK Mom, I understand, but ...**
5   **Mom! Look Mom, you've got to get a life! What? No, I'm not**
6   **hanging up on you.**
7   **MICHELLE:** *(Enters.)* **Hey, Alan!**
8   **ALAN: Hey, Michelle!**
9   **MICHELLE: I'm sorry, were you talking to someone?**
10   **ALAN:** *(Moves phone away from his ear.)* **No, just finished**
11   **talking. So, what are you doing?**
12   **MICHELLE: Same as you. Buying school supplies. You know, it**
13   **was easier when all we had to buy were pencils, crayons,**
14   **scissors, gluc, and a ruler.**
15   **ALAN: And don't forget that important box of tissues!**
16   **MICHELLE: Yes, twenty boxes of tissues stacked in one corner.**
17   **We always used them, though. Well, I better get busy.**
18   **Unfortunately, my list is not so elementary anymore.**
19   *(Exits.)*
20   **ALAN: See ya.** *(Suddenly remembers his mother is still on the*
21   *phone.)* **Mom, are you still there?** *(Quickly pulls phone*
22   *away from ear to indicate she is screaming.)* **Mom, I'm sorry.**
23   **What do you expect me to do, talk to you instead of my**
24   **friends? Look, why don't you go take a nap or something?**
25   **And when you wake up, I'll be home ... Mom, are we going**
26   **to have to go through this every single time?**
27   **TYLER:** *(Enters.)* **Hey, Alan. You buying school supplies, too?**

1   ALAN: *(Puts phone down.)* **Yeah.**

2   TYLER: **Look, I've got pages of school supplies from six**
3   **different teachers! How am I supposed to figure all this**
4   **out?**

5   ALAN: **Welcome to high school.**

6   TYLER: *(Looking at the list)* **You know, I can understand index**
7   **cards, graph paper, colored pencils, and a compass, but**
8   **why the heck do we need a supply box?**

9   ALAN: **Who's the teacher?**

10 TYLER: *(Looking)* **Mrs. Griffin. English.**

11 ALAN: **Oh, she's the teacher who has her room decorated like**
12   **a kindergarten class. She probably wishes she was**
13   **teaching elementary, but somehow got stuck in high**
14   **school.**

15 TYLER: **Great! Like I want to carry my G.I. Joe supply box to**
16   **her room everyday.**

17 ALAN: **I think she lets you leave it in the class as long as your**
18   **name is on the box.**

19 TYLER: **Great. Can't wait. But there is one thing I miss about**
20   **buying school supplies.**

21 ALAN: **What's that?**

22 TYLER: **Picking out that special lunchbox. You know, like**
23   **Batman or Spiderman. Or the Hulk! Remember how**
24   **much fun it was to show off your new lunchbox to all your**
25   **friends?**

26 ALAN: **Yeah. I had a cool Superman lunchbox.**

27 TYLER: **Well, so much for the good old days.**

28 ALAN: **But now we get to leave the campus for lunch.**

29 TYLER: **If you have a car! Oh, that's right. You have a car now,**
30   **don't you?**

31 ALAN: *(Proudly)* **As of yesterday.**

32 TYLER: **Man, you're lucky.**

33 ALAN: *(Looks at his phone.)* **I guess.**

34 TYLER: **Well, I better go find this stuff. Bye.** *(Exits.)*

35 ALAN: *(Into the phone)* **Mom, are you still there? ... I'm sorry! I**

1   was talking to Tyler ... Oh, well I'm glad you heard my

2   entire conversation! So, can I let you go now? ... Why not?

3   Mom!

4   SALESMAN: *(Enters.)* Sir, may I help you?

5   ALAN: *(Puts phone down.)* No, I was just looking for some

6   school supplies.

7   SALESMAN: Can I help you find anything in particular?

8   ALAN: *(Pulls out a long list.)* All this.

9   SALESMAN: Looks like you'll need a cart. I'll be right back.

10 ALAN: *(Into the phone)* Mom, are you still there? ... I'm sorry! I

11   know you're worried, but I'm here at the store! You heard

12   me talking to the salesman! Can I just let you go and see

13   you when I get home? ... Mom, of course you'll see me

14   again! ... No, I'm not going to have a wreck and die! ... Mom!

15 MICHELLE: *(Enters.)* Hey, Alan. Have you seen the pocket

16   folders with brads?

17 ALAN: *(Puts phone down and turns to MICHELLE.)* No, I haven't

18   seen them. Sorry.

19 MICHELLE: Gosh, you don't have any supplies yet.

20 ALAN: Yeah, I guess I'm slow.

21 MICHELLE: Well, you better get busy or you'll be here all night!

22 ALAN: *(Into the phone)* Is that what you want? For me to stay

23   here all night?

24 MICHELLE: Uh ... is everything OK?

25 ALAN: *(Puts phone down.)* Yeah, I was just have a little fight.

26 MICHELLE: With your girlfriend?

27 ALAN: With my mom.

28 MICHELLE: Is everything OK?

29 ALAN: No, not really. See, I got my first car yesterday and today

30   I finally get to drive all the way to the store by myself!

31 MICHELLE: That's great!

32 ALAN: Not when your mom calls every two seconds to find out

33   if you're still alive!

34 MICHELLE: Every two seconds?

35 ALAN: You'd think I was in elementary! I feel like I should be

1   buying crayons the way she's treating me! So much for
2   getting a car and being independent!
3 MICHELLE: That would be irritating. And embarrassing.
4 ALAN: Oh, it is embarrassing! *(Imitating his mother's voice)* **Where**
5   **are you now? And now where are you? Did you remember to**
6   **stop and look both ways before crossing the street? Are you**
7   **wearing your seat belt? Where are you now? You don't have**
8   **the radio on, do you? You're not speeding, are you? And**
9   **where are you now?** *(Shaking the phone)* **She's driving me**
10   **crazy!**
11 MICHELLE: I'm sorry. It'd drive me crazy, too. You know, you
12   could always turn your phone off.
13 ALAN: Turn my phone off?
14 MICHELLE: Sure, why not?
15 ALAN: Why didn't I think of that? Hey, you want to have lunch
16   sometime?
17 MICHELLE: Sure!
18 ALAN: Tomorrow?
19 MICHELLE: Yeah! That'd be nice.
20 ALAN: Then it's a date. OK, I guess I better get back to my
21   shopping.
22 MICHELLE: Good luck! And remember my advice. Just turn the
23   phone off! *(Exits.)*
24 ALAN: Yeah. Just turn the phone off. *(Suddenly remembers his*
25   *Mom is still on the phone.)* **Mom, are you still there? ...** *(Pulls*
26   *phone away from ear.)* **Mom, quit yelling at me. Mom! I'm**
27   **sorry! Look, you've got to stop worrying! I'm practically an**
28   **adult!** *(Pulls phone away from ear, then after a pause, smiles.)*
29   **Mom ... Mom ... Mom, you're breaking up on me. Hello! Mom?**
30   **I think I'm standing in a dead zone. Mom?** *(Smiling, he hangs*
31   *up the phone.)* **Sorry, Mom, but you know how those dead**
32   **zones are. And what's this? My battery is low? I better keep**
33   **my phone off in case I need it for an emergency.** *(Smiles and*
34   *takes the keys from his pocket and shakes them.)* **Yes!**

Last Free Summer

Cast (2 Male, 2 Female): Jed, Neil, Allison, Katy

.

1　　*(AT RISE: JED, NEIL, ALLISON, and KATY are sitting in the*
2　　*grass on a hot summer day.)*
3　**JED:** I wish I had my driver's license. Six more months.
4　**NEIL:** Only four months for me.
5　**ALLISON:** *(Counting on her fingers)* Five for me.
6　**KATY:** Seven here.
7　**JED:** And then next year, I won't be sitting around all summer
8　　doing nothing!
9　**NEIL:** To the pool!
10　**ALLISON:** Off to the mall!
11　**KATY:** Anywhere we want to go! That is, if we have a car.
12　**ALLISON:** My mom says I have to get a job if I want a car.
13　**KATY:** Have our moms been talking?
14　**NEIL:** Yeah my dad says, "Son, don't think we're just going to
15　　hand you a car and turn you loose. You're going to have to
16　　take that next step in becoming an adult by getting a job.
17　　Son, cars are expensive. Not only do you have a car payment,
18　　but insurance, car tags, inspection stickers, oil changes, not
19　　to mention gas. And you know how expensive gas is these
20　　days! And, if I might add, when you least expect it, the
21　　battery dies, or you need new tires, or something else goes
22　　wrong. And, son, repairs are not cheap!"
23　**JED:** Yeah, I got a similar speech. It's like they're trying to depress
24　　us before we even get a car.
25　**KATY:** You'd think our parents wanted us to stay kids and ride
26　　our bikes.
27　**ALLISON:** Why do they have to take the fun out of getting our
28　　first car? And since I got my driver's permit, my mom is
29　　always so reluctant to let me drive. Tell me, how am I

1   supposed to learn if she's always too nervous to let me
2   drive?
3   KATY: Well, when I drive, my mom holds onto the dashboard
4   with a look of panic on her face. And she's always saying,
5   "Slow down! Slow down!" And I'm not even going fast.
6   JED: Well, at least next summer we won't be sitting around
7   here doing nothing.
8   KATY: That's right! We'll be out on the town!
9   ALLISON: The mall, the movies ... anywhere we want to go!
10 NEIL: That is, after I get off work.
11 JED: Yeah, my parents will make me get a job, too. *(Imitating*
12   *his father)* "Because son, cars are expensive to maintain!"
13 KATY: I'll have to get a job, too.
14 ALLISON: Same here.
15 KATY: You know, when you think about it, this is our last free
16   summer.
17 JED: You're right, Katy. And all this time I was thinking about
18   how next summer I'd have all the freedom in the world.
19   Guess not. Guess we'll all be working.
20 ALLISON: Yuck.
21 JED: Double yuck.
22 KATY: So what are we doing here? We need to have some fun
23   before it's too late!
24 NEIL: Yeah, because next summer, we won't have time for
25   anything, except work!
26 ALLISON: You're right, Katy. This is our last free summer to
27   hang out and have fun. And you know, it's sad. We've all
28   grown up in this neighborhood and have always had so
29   much fun riding our bikes ...
30 JED: Camping out in our yards.
31 NEIL: Walking to the park.
32 ALLISON: Having those silly lemonade stands.
33 JED: Remember those water balloon fights?
34 KATY: And remember my Slip and Slide?
35 NEIL: And that hill we'd climb in the alley! Man, a couple of

1   years ago, that hill looked huge!

2 JED: Yeah, it kinda shrunk.

3 ALLISON: And Katy and I had Barbie swimming parties.

4 KATY: *(Laughing)* **In the neighbor's birdbath!**

5 ALLISON: And remember when we'd collect insects and
6   pretend they were our Barbies' pets?

7 KATY: And that time we gave our Barbies a haircut!

8 ALLISON: Yeah, we spent hours and hours just playing with
9   those stupid Barbies.

10 KATY: I still have mine.

11 ALLISON: Me, too.

12 JED: Yeah, those were the good old days.

13 NEIL: Hey, if this is our last summer to hang out and have fun,
14   then we need to do what we used to do and have some fun!

15 JED: You're right!

16 NEIL: So Jed, you wanna go climb that hill in the alley?

17 JED: *(Jumps up.)* **Let's see who can get there first!** *(JED and NEIL*
18   *run Off.)*

19 KATY: So ... do you want to play Barbies?

20 ALLISON: I'll get mine if you get yours.

21 KATY: *(Stands.)* **I'm on my way.**

22 ALLISON: *(Stands.)* **Hey, don't forget that Barbie camper.**

23 KATY: OK! And I'll bring us a blanket to sit on.

24 ALLISON: And I'll bring a sack lunch.

25 KATY: Great! See you back here in a minute!

26 ALLISON: OK! *(They exit.)*

Un-Identical Twins

Cast (1 Male, 3 Female): Mom, Dad, Nicole, Gertrude
Setting: Kitchen.

.

1 MOM: *(Calling out)* Nicole, sweetheart, would you come into
2   the kitchen please?
3 DAD: Is this your annual pep talk?
4 MOM: Yes, but I plan to handle it a bit differently this year.
5 DAD: Care to fill me in?
6 MOM: Just follow my lead.
7 DAD: Well, I'd like to know what direction we're going.
8 MOM: George, next week is their first day at a new school, and
9   I want to help them get off to a good start.
10 DAD: Them?
11 MOM: I thought with a little advice, this year might be better.
12 DAD: Honey, I know you don't want to deal with a daughter
13   coming home in tears everyday, but I don't know how a
14   little advice is going to help.
15 MOM: Well, I have to try.
16 DAD: You know, I'll never understand how we managed to
17   have twin daughters who are completely different. I
18   mean, they don't look or act alike in the least!
19 MOM: Like night and day.
20 DAD: The pretty one and the ... what should we say?
21 MOM: Don't say it. We can't call our own daughter a geek.
22 DAD: Well, it's the truth.
23 MOM: You know, I keep hoping she'll grow out of it.
24 DAD: After sixteen years, I don't think that's going to happen.
25 MOM: Poor Nicole.
26 DAD: Poor Nicole? She's the beautiful daughter!
27 MOM: Poor Nicole because she always has to feel bad for her
28   twin sister.

1 NICOLE: *(Enters.)* What about me feeling bad for my sister?

2 MOM: We mean you feel sorry for your sister.

3 NICOLE: Of course I do! With that name you gave her, who

4   wouldn't feel sorry for her? You know, Mom, Dad, that's

5   probably the reason my sister is such a geek.

6 DAD: Because of her name?

7 NICOLE: Yes! How could anyone grow up feeling beautiful

8   with that name? Gertrude. Nicole, now that's beautiful.

9   But Gertrude?

10 MOM: But I thought it was a pretty name.

11 DAD: It was your great-grandmother's name.

12 NICOLE: I know. But thank you for having some sense when

13   you named me. Nicole's a pretty name, isn't it?

14 MOM: George, I think Nicole is right. It's our fault for giving

15   Gertrude such an old-fashioned name. What were we

16   thinking?

17 DAD: Maybe there's some truth to it.

18 NICOLE: You know Mom, it may be too late, but you could

19   always change her name.

20 MOM: George, do you suppose we could?

21 DAD: I don't know.

22 NICOLE: It might help her come out of her shell. *(GERTRUDE*

23   *enters. Her hair and clothes are a mess. She walks with her*

24   *head down, bumping into the kitchen table.)*

25 GERTRUDE: Good morning, Mother. Good morning, Father.

26 MOM: Sweetheart, come sit down. Here, let me push that hair

27   out of your face. You know you have such a pretty face.

28 GERTRUDE: My twin sister got the pretty face, not me.

29 DAD: Gertrude, that's not true.

30 GERTRUDE: Yes it is.

31 NICOLE: She's right, Dad.

32 GERTRUDE: Everyone says Nicole is the pretty twin and I'm

33   the ugly one.

34 MOM: Now, now that's enough. Sweetheart, are you hungry?

35 GERTRUDE: Yes. Can I have three pancakes, three eggs, some

1   bacon, and a bowl of cereal? I'm hungry!

2 MOM: How about a protein bar instead? Doesn't that sound
3   nutritious?

4 GERTRUDE: No. Mom, do you think I'm fat?

5 MOM: Sweetheart, no! Of course not! I just want my precious
6   daughter to be healthy.

7 GERTRUDE: But I don't like protein bars.

8 NICOLE: Here, I'll take it, Mom.

9 MOM: Then how about some oatmeal?

10 GERTRUDE: How about a few cookies instead?

11 MOM: Sweetheart, I don't think that's a good breakfast.

12 GERTRUDE: Then fix me some pancakes!

13 NICOLE: Mom, are you going to tell her?

14 GERTRUDE: Tell me what?

15 MOM: Well, sweetheart, your father and I have this idea ...

16 NICOLE: Actually, it was my idea.

17 DAD: And sweetheart, it's only an idea. If you don't like it, we
18   don't have to do it.

19 GERTRUDE: What? You want to give me up for adoption?

20 MOM: Sweetheart, no! Why would you say such a silly thing?

21 GERTRUDE: Because you're embarrassed to have me as a
22   daughter.

23 DAD: Gertrude, that's not true.

24 GERTRUDE: Nicole is pretty and I'm ugly. I don't even look
25   like I belong to this family.

26 DAD: That's not true.

27 GERTRUDE: Yes it is. I'm ugly and all the kids at school call me
28   the Ugly Duckling.

29 MOM: But that's what our idea is about.

30 GERTRUDE: It's OK, Mom. You can give me away.

31 DAD: Gertrude, we're not trying to give you away.

32 MOM: Sweetheart, what I'm trying to say is that we want to
33   give you a new name.

34 GERTRUDE: A new name?

35 DAD: That's right. We realized that we made a mistake by

1   giving you such an old-fashioned name. After all, what girl
2   wants to be named Gertrude?
3   GERTRUDE: I do. I like my name.
4   MOM: But Sweetheart, wouldn't you like to have a different
5   name?
6   GERTRUDE: No.
7   DAD: Any name that you want? I can have my attorney do the
8   papers for a name change.
9   GERTRUDE: It's OK, Dad. I'll keep my name. Unless ...
10   MOM: Unless what?
11   GERTRUDE: My new parents want to change it.
12   MOM: Gertrude, we are not giving you up for adoption!
13   NICOLE: How about the name Sophia? Remember how you
14   used to always name your dolls that? And you know, it
15   does sound glamorous.
16   GERTRUDE: Well ...
17   MOM: Oh, I think that's pretty.
18   GERTRUDE: I do like that name.
19   MOM: You do?
20   GERTRUDE: Uh-huh.
21   DAD: Well, why don't we try it out? How about if you leave and
22   walk back in and we'll call you Sophia. See how it feels.
23   GERTRUDE: Well, OK. *(Bumps into things as she exits.)*
24   DAD: *(Calling out)* Sophia, time for breakfast!
25   GERTRUDE: *(Enters.)* I liked that. Can I try it again?
26   DAD: You bet. *(GERTRUDE exits.)*
27   NICOLE: I think it's working.
28   MOM: I think so, too.
29   DAD: And to think, all this time it was our fault for giving her
30   such an uncommon name.
31   MOM: How could we have done that?
32   DAD: What were we thinking?
33   NICOLE: At least you were thinking when you named me. I
34   love my name. Nicole. It's pretty, isn't it?
35   MOM: Yes, sweetheart. Just like you.

1   NICOLE: Thanks, Mom.

2   DAD: OK, let's call her back in.

3   MOM: Let me try it. *(Calling out)* **Sophia! Oh, Sophia!**

4   GERTRUDE: *(She has changed shirts, her hair is combed, and*

5   *she enters the room smiling with a confident look and a*

6   *graceful walk.)* **Good morning! Good morning everyone!**

7   MOM: Oh, Sweetheart! You look ... you look beautiful!

8   DAD: Wow. What a transformation.

9   GERTRUDE: Thank you. From now on, just call me Sophia.

10   You like, twin sister?

11 NICOLE: Excuse me, but that's my shirt you're wearing!

12 MOM: Now Nicole, be sweet. Sisters need to share.

13 NICOLE: Mom!

14 GERTRUDE: And you know what, I'm through hiding behind

15   my twin sister. From now on, I'm a new person!

16 MOM: Gertrude ...

17 GERTRUDE: It's Sophia, remember?

18 MOM: Sophia, there's no need to be rude.

19 GERTRUDE: I'm sorry, mother.

20 MOM: Would you like for us to buy you some new clothes to go

21   with your new name?

22 GERTRUDE: Yes, thank you! And could I put some highlights

23   in my hair, too?

24 MOM: Of course, sweetheart.

25 DAD: I still can't believe my eyes. All because of a name

26   change.

27 NICOLE: I'm not sure I like it!

28 GERTRUDE: I know, because now you have to worry about me

29   outshining you. But if you ever feel depressed, you can cry

30   on my shoulder.

31 NICOLE: Mom!

32 MOM: Oh, she's just excited.

33 NICOLE: Excited? She's turned into a snob!

34 GERTRUDE: Yes, this school year will be different. A new

35   school, a new name, new clothes, new friends ... I'll

1   probably be the most popular girl there!
2   NICOLE: Maybe second most popular.
3   GERTRUDE: No, *the* most popular!
4   NICOLE: Not more than me!
5   GERTRUDE: Watch me!
6   MOM: Girls, girls!
7   NICOLE: Gee, I hope I don't forget and call you by your *real*
8   name!
9   GERTRUDE: Well, if you do, I'll just ignore you.
10   MOM: Gertrude.
11   GERTRUDE: *Mom!*
12   MOM: I mean, Sophia ...
13   NICOLE: Gertrude, Gertrude, Gertrude, *Gertrude*!
14   GERTRUDE: Sophia, Sophia, Sophia, *Sophia*!
15   DAD: Girls! Please!
16   NICOLE: Mom!
17   MOM: Nicole, just be patient. We all need time to get used to
18   her name.
19   DAD: Sophia, you do look beautiful.
20   MOM: Yes, you're like a bright shining star.
21   GERTRUDE: Thank you, Father. Thank you, Mother.
22   NICOLE: Well, I liked the other idea better!
23   MOM: What other idea?
24   NICOLE: Give her up for adoption! *Please!*

Plays for
Five Actors

Ditto

Cast (3 Male, 2 Female): Sara, Travis, Eddie, Jay, Kelly

Prop: Class ring.

1 SHELLY: Travis, Travis, wait up!

2 TRAVIS: Hey, Shelly. What's up?

3 SHELLY: Do you have a minute?

4 TRAVIS: Sure. I was just headed home to do homework. You

5 know Mr. Watkins who runs his math class like the

6 military? Well, today he gave the class two hundred extra

7 problems because someone was talking. Wasn't me, but

8 we all got punished. So, I need to get home and finish so I

9 can spend the evening with Kelly.

10 SHELLY: Speaking of Kelly ...

11 TRAVIS: My beautiful bride to be!

12 SHELLY: Bride to be? You're engaged?

13 TRAVIS: Not officially, but in our hearts we are. Last week

14 when we celebrated our three-month anniversary, we

15 promised to love each other forever! *(EDDIE enters and*

16 *listens.)*

17 SHELLY: Kelly said she wanted to marry you?

18 TRAVIS: If I might quote her, "Travis, my heart will be yours

19 forever. And I can't wait until the day that I become your

20 wife."

21 SHELLY: She said that?

22 TRAVIS: She said that!

23 EDDIE: Are you serious? You're engaged?

24 TRAVIS: Oh hi, Eddie. Yes, we're practically engaged.

25 EDDIE: Did you give her a ring?

26 TRAVIS: Yes, of course I did!

27 EDDIE: You did?

28 TRAVIS: Yes I did! *(EDDIE hums the wedding march.)*

1   SHELLY: Eddie, shut up! *(Holds up a class ring.)* **A class ring is**
2   **not an engagement ring!**
3   TRAVIS: **Hey, what are you doing with my ring? I gave that to**
4   **Kelly!**
5   SHELLY: **Well, Kelly asked me to give it back to you.**
6   EDDIE: **Uh-oh!**
7   TRAVIS: **Why?**
8   SHELLY: **Listen, don't get upset ...**
9   EDDIE: **Dude, I think your fiancée is calling off the**
10   **engagement.**
11 TRAVIS: *(To SHELLY)* **Is that what she's doing?**
12 SHELLY: **I hate to be the bearer of bad news.**
13 TRAVIS: **Tell me! Just tell me!**
14 JAY: *(Enters.)* **Hey guys. What's up?**
15 TRAVIS: **Tell me, Shelly!**
16 JAY: **Tell you what?**
17 EDDIE: **Kelly is calling off their engagement.**
18 JAY: **You two were engaged? Man! I can't believe that!**
19 SHELLY: **They weren't engaged!**
20 TRAVIS: **Yes we were! Last week, when we celebrated our**
21   **three-month anniversary, we promised to get married.**
22 JAY: **Wow. When?**
23 EDDIE: **Drop it, Jay. Kelly called off the engagement.**
24 JAY: **Gosh, I'm sorry.**
25 SHELLY: **They weren't engaged!**
26 EDDIE: **Well, if they were, they aren't now.**
27 SHELLY: **They weren't!**
28 TRAVIS: **So, what'd she say? Huh? Tell me every single word!**
29 JAY: **Why is it that girls always send their best friend to do their**
30   **dirty work?**
31 TRAVIS: **Yeah, why didn't she want to tell me herself? Maybe**
32   **it's because you're lying!**
33 SHELLY: **If I were lying, why would I be holding your class ring**
34   **that she gave me to give back to you?** *(TRAVIS snatches the*
35   *ring from her hand.)*

74

1   JAY: Man, it's OK. We'll help you through this.

2   EDDIE: Yeah, you can count on us.

3   TRAVIS: OK, Shelly! Tell me! Why did she do this?

4   SHELLY: Well, Kelly felt like you were becoming too serious,
5   and it scared her.

6   TRAVIS: Well, she was as serious as I was! She wanted to get
7   married as much as I did!

8   EDDIE: Guess she changed her mind.

9   JAY: Man, it'll be OK.

10   TRAVIS: But we were in love! We were going to get married!

11   SHELLY: She still wants to be friends.

12   TRAVIS: Friends? *Friends?* I can't be friends after this!

13   JAY: Man, I don't blame you.

14   EDDIE: Just walk away. Act as if you could care less.

15   TRAVIS: I can't believe this! We have five classes together and
16   now I have to ignore my fiancée! You know, this is going to
17   be a little hard! One day you're sitting in History class in
18   love and planning to get married and the next day you
19   can't even lean over and ask to borrow a pen! This is just
20   great!

21   JAY: Travis, we'll help you through this.

22   EDDIE: Yeah, you'll be fine. You'll be over her like that. *(Snaps.)*

23   SHELLY: Look, I'm sorry. But I'm just the messenger.

24   JAY: Yeah, it's not her fault, Travis.

25   EDDIE: You can't blame Shelly.

26   TRAVIS: Well, maybe I want you to give her a message from
27   me!

28   JAY: Good idea, Travis.

29   EDDIE: Yeah, tell her thanks because it saved you from
30   breaking up with her.

31   TRAVIS: Tell her ... tell her ... *(Begins to cry.)* Tell her that I still
32   love her! Forever and ever and ever ...

33   EDDIE: Oh, no! You don't want to tell her that!

34   JAY: Man, have some pride!

35   TRAVIS: *(Still crying)* But I do still love her! I really do! Oh,

1   Kelly, oh baby, please come back to me! Remember how
2   we were going to love each other forever? Forever and
3   forever and forever ...
4   JAY: Man, you've gotta get a grip!
5   EDDIE: Come on; let's go play some ball. Let's get out of here.
6   SHELLY: So, do you have a message for me to give her? *(TRAVIS*
7   *shakes his head.)*
8   EDDIE: That's the way! You show her you could care less!
9   JAY: That's right. It's time to move on.
10 TRAVIS: I know. I can do this.
11 JAY: *(To SHELLY)* Tell Kelly that Travis said "Ditto."
12 SHELLY: OK. Ditto. *(She exits.)*
13 EDDIE: Good idea, Jay. Come on, Travis, we're getting you out
14   of here.
15 TRAVIS: But I really did love her!
16 JAY: We know, but in time, it'll get easier.
17 TRAVIS: I wish that time would hurry up and get here!
18 JAY: Hey, by tomorrow, you'll hardly even remember her
19   name.
20 EDDIE: Jay's right.
21 TRAVIS: I hope so.
22 KELLY: *(Rushing over to TRAVIS)* Travis!
23 EDDIE: *(To TRAVIS)* Act like you don't care.
24 JAY: Yeah, be cool.
25 TRAVIS: *(Trying to be strong)* Yes Kelly? What is it?
26 KELLY: Ditto? You wanted to break up, too?
27 EDDIE: He sure did!
28 JAY: Saved him the trouble, Kelly.
29 KELLY: Well, you could've told me yourself!
30 JAY: Like you did?
31 EDDIE: Besides, he was just about to tell you when Shelly
32   showed up with the wonderful news.
33 KELLY: Wonderful news?!
34 JAY: But if you hadn't done it, he was definitely going to do it! Right,
35   Travis?

1   **TRAVIS: Yeah, right. I ... I ... Oh, Kelly ...**

2   **JAY: Man, hold it together. You can do it. Remember, she just**

3   **dumped you.**

4   **EDDIE: Be strong, Travis. Make us proud.**

5   **KELLY: What? Were you about to say something?**

6   **TRAVIS:** *(Looks at JAY and EDDIE.)* **I sure was.** *(Puts the ring back on*

7   *his hand.)* **Ditto!**

8   **KELLY: Well, ditto to you, too, you jerk!** *(She runs off.)*

9   **TRAVIS:** *(Holding out his arms)* **Oh Kelly, come back!**

10   **JAY:** *(Forcing his arms down)* **Man, don't do that!**

11   **EDDIE: Control yourself. You're going to be OK.**

12   **TRAVIS: But I loved her!**

13   **JAY: And you'll love again.**

14   **TRAVIS: You think so?**

15   **JAY: Absolutely!**

16   **EDDIE: Come on, let's go play some ball.** *(They start off, but Travis*

17   *stops and turns around.)*

18   **JAY: Hey, don't look back!**

19   **TRAVIS: OK, OK. Did you know I was going to let you guys be my**

20   **groomsmen?**

21   **JAY:** *(Lightly hits his head.)* **Forget about her.**

22   **SHELLY:** *(Enters.)* **Hey, Travis, wait up!**

23   **TRAVIS: What now, Shelly?**

24   **SHELLY: Well, when Kelly found out you were going to break up**

25   **with her, well, it just broke her heart and well ... she said she**

26   **still loves you.**

27   **TRAVIS: She does?**

28   **EDDIE:** *(Shaking his head)* **What is it with girls?**

29   **JAY: They're a basket case, that's for sure!**

30   **SHELLY: Yes, she still loves you. So, do you have a message for her?**

31   **TRAVIS: Yes! Oh yes! Tell her I said** *ditto*! *(JAY and EDDIE shake*

32   *their heads. SHELLY exits. TRAVIS is ecstatic as the boys escort*

33   *him Off.)*

A New Style

Cast (5 Female): Ann, Dana, Holly, Kim, Melanie

·

1 ANN: Dana, what did you do to your hair?

2 DANA: It looks terrible, doesn't it?

3 ANN: It's short.

4 DANA: I thought if I cut it, it'd make me look more ... you know,

5   more mature. You hate it don't you?

6 ANN: No, it's just ... I'm just not used to it! I mean, since first

7   grade your hair has been to your waist. Now it's ... it's

8   short!

9 DANA: Oh, I wish I hadn't cut it!

10 ANN: It'll grow back.

11 DANA: From here to my waist? That'll take years! Oh, I hate it!

12   I just hate it!

13 ANN: I think it's cute.

14 DANA: You're lying. Please don't lie to me.

15 ANN: OK.

16 DANA: So you hate it, don't you?

17 ANN: Hate is an awfully strong word. I'd say ... I'd say ...

18 DANA: Say it! Just say it!

19 ANN: It's different.

20 DANA: Bad different or good different?

21 ANN: Neither. Just different.

22 HOLLY: *(Enters.)* Dana, you cut your hair! Oh, my gosh! Why

23   did you cut it? It was so long and pretty! I would've done

24   anything to have your hair! You cut it? You really cut it?

25 ANN: And doesn't it make her look more mature? *(Elbows*

26   *HOLLY.)*

27 HOLLY: Not really. But, I do think it makes her look more ...

28   more ... what's the word?

29 DANA: More what? Say it! Just say it!

1   ANN: Sophisticated!

2   HOLLY: No, that's not it.

3   ANN: Elegant!

4   HOLLY: No, not that.

5   ANN: Glamorous!

6   HOLLY: No.

7   ANN: Stylish!

8   HOLLY: No.

9   DANA: Then *what*?

10   HOLLY: Plain.

11   DANA: *Plain?*

12   ANN: *Holly!*

13   HOLLY: Well, I'm being honest! You want me to be honest,
14   don't you? Before, Dana always got lots of attention
15   because her hair was long. I mean, how many people have
16   long hair nowadays? Not too many. And now she just looks
17   like everyone else. Plain.

18   DANA: I hate it! I just hate it!

19   HOLLY: It'll grow back.

20   DANA: Maybe I should get a wig!

21   HOLLY: Too bad you can't get all your hair back and glue it on.

22   DANA: I wish I could!

23   HOLLY: Oh well. We live, we learn.

24   ANN: Well, I'm starting to like it more and more. And yes, I do
25   think you look more mature. Who wants to look like a
26   little girl with long hair?

27   HOLLY: I'd take long hair. I'm just not patient enough to let it
28   grow out. It always gets to a certain point, and then I'm
29   running off to the salon for a new style.

30   ANN: And now Dana has a great new style! It was time. Time to
31   grow up and cut the little girl hair off.

32   DANA: You really think so, Ann?

33   ANN: Absolutely! And I really like your cut. I wouldn't mind
34   getting one just like it. Of course it probably wouldn't look
35   as good on me.

1   HOLLY: Anything would look better on you than those stupid
2   ponytails you always wear. Talk about needing a new style!
3   ANN: Well, look who's talking! You with the split ends!
4   HOLLY: I don't have split ends!
5   ANN: Well, maybe you should look a little closer! And Dana,
6   your hair looks so healthy now. It's not weighed down, but
7   bouncy and shiny!
8   DANA: You really like it?
9   ANN: I'm liking it more and more every minute!
10 DANA: Really?
11 ANN: Really.
12 HOLLY: Can I disagree?
13 ANN: Holly, why don't you take your negativity and split ends
14   somewhere else?
15 HOLLY: Fine! *(Exits.)*
16 ANN: She is the most negative person I ever met! I think she's
17   jealous!
18 DANA: Jealous? Of me?
19 ANN: Of course! Look how stylish you are now! She's the one
20   who's plain! But you ... Wow! You're radiant!
21 DANA: Really?
22 ANN: Really!
23 KIM: *(Enters.)* Whoa! What happened to you?
24 ANN: *(Quickly)* Well, Dana decided she was tired of looking like
25   a little schoolgirl and cut her hair. Now she looks
26   glamorous!
27 KIM: *(Walking around her)* Wow ...
28 ANN: Like a model!
29 KIM: *(Still circling her)* Wow ...
30 DANA: Kim, would you say something? Please!
31 KIM: Wow. I can't believe you cut your hair.
32 ANN: *(Nodding to KIM)* And doesn't it look great?
33 KIM: *(Noticing ANN)* Oh yeah. Yeah, it looks great!
34 DANA: So you like it?
35 KIM: Yeah, it's so ... so ... so ...

1   DANA: What?

2   KIM: It's so you!

3   DANA: Really?

4   KIM: Yeah! It's short and cute and it draws attention to your
5   face. And now your eyes stand out more! I mean, before all
6   you could see was your long old hair, but now it's all about
7   your face! Your beautiful eyes, your high cheekbones ...
8   Wow ... that's all I can say.

9   DANA: Thanks, Kim. I thought I'd like a new style and now ...
10   now I'm sure I do! Thanks Kim!

11 MELANIE: *(Enters.)* Dana! Dana! What happened to your hair?

12 DANA: *(Smiling)* Like it?

13 MELANIE: You cut your beautiful hair?

14 DANA: Yes, to draw more attention to my face. *(A huge smile)*
15   Like it?

16 MELANIE: But your hair ... I loved your hair!

17 DANA: And now you can notice my face! *(Bats eyes.)*

18 MELANIE: But your hair ...

19 ANN: And now Dana is glamorous and stylish!

20 MELANIE: But your hair!

21 KIM: And don't you just love it?

22 MELANIE: No, I hate it!

23 DANA: *(Smile disappears.)* You hate it?

24 MELANIE: *(Noticing ANN and KIM who are giving her "the
25   look.")* Yes, I mean no, I mean ...

26 DANA: What do you mean? You hate it or you don't? Oh, I knew
27   it! Everyone's going to hate it! I hate it, too! Oh, I wish I'd
28   never cut my hair!

29 MELANIE: No, no, I mean I hate it that you look so good!

30 DANA: What?

31 MELANIE: What can I say? I'm jealous.

32 DANA: Really? You're jealous?

33 MELANIE: I hate to admit it.

34 DANA: Buy why?

35 MELANIE: Why?

1   DANA: Yes, why?

2   MELANIE: Why?

3   DANA: Yes! Why?

4   MELANIE: Why? Because ...

5   KIM: Why do you think, Dana? Because now you look so

6   beautiful and you make the rest of us look rather blah.

7   *(Pointing to each of them)* **Blah ... blah ... blah!**

8   MELANIE: Uh, yeah? *(To KIM)* **Blah?**

9   KIM: We're over here looking all drab and you ... you are so

10   cute!

11 DANA: Really?

12 ANN: It's true.

13 MELANIE: *(To KIM)* **Blah?**

14 DANA: Well, I do like it. I mean, at first I didn't know, but now

15   I'm getting used to it, and I really do like it.

16 KIM: You know, you can always let it grow back out if you

17   change your mind. And I heard that your hair grows faster

18   after it's been cut.

19 ANN: And faster in the summer. Something about the heat, I

20   guess.

21 KIM: I heard that, too.

22 MELANIE: So, if you're lucky, it'll be back where it was before

23   you know it!

24 DANA: If I'm lucky?

25 MELANIE: I mean ...

26 ANN: She means you're lucky that your hair grows so fast and

27   you have so many choices.

28 MELANIE: Yeah.

29 DANA: But I thought I'd keep it short like this. You know, to

30   bring out my eyes.

31 KIM: And I think you should.

32 ANN: Me too.

33 MELANIE: Sure. Whatever you like, we like! *(They all smile at*

34   *DANA.)*

35 DANA: *(Looks at them.)* **Oh, you all hate it, don't you?** *(They force*

1   *a smile and give a small nod.)* **Oh, I hate it, too!** *(Runs Off*
2   *crying.)*
3   **MELANIE:** *(After a short pause)* **At least it'll grow back!** *(The*
4   *girls nod.)*

Teen Night

Cast (2 Male, 3 Female): Grandma, Cindy,
Jason, Randy, Lindsey
Prop: Restaurant menu.
Setting: A café.

1   *(AT RISE: GRANDMA and CINDY enter. GRANDMA is*
2   *looking around.)*
3   GRANDMA: So, this is the hangout?
4   CINDY: *(Leading GRANDMA to a table)* Grandma, why don't
5   you sit down right here and relax. I'll come back and
6   check on you in a little while, OK?
7   GRANDMA: Wait! Where are you going?
8   CINDY: I'll just be right over there talking to my friends,
9   OK?
10 GRANDMA: But I want to come with you!
11 CINDY: Grandma, I understand that you want to hang out
12   with me, but really, you'll just be bored.
13 GRANDMA: I won't be bored!
14 CINDY: *(Hands GRANDMA a menu.)* Here, take this menu
15   and order something to eat. Take your time and just
16   relax, OK? And I'll be back to check on you.
17 GRANDMA: *(Puts the menu down.)* Cindy, when I was your
18   age, your grandma was the life of the party!
19 CINDY: I'm sure, Grandma. *(Opens the menu.)* Here, look at
20   this menu. See something you want to order?
21 GRANDMA: Well, it's true. And don't you think for a minute
22   that I've lost that fun spirit just because I'm a little
23   older. Because believe me, I still know how to party!
24 CINDY: *(Putting the menu in her face)* Grandma, aren't you
25   hungry?
26 GRANDMA: Sure. Let's order some fries.

1   **CINDY:** I thought you didn't eat stuff like that. You know,
2   your cholesterol.
3   **GRANDMA:** Look, Cindy, I'm seventy-two years old, and I'm
4   tired of staying home and knitting and taking naps.
5   Life is short! I don't know how much time I've got left,
6   but I want to live it up! Starting tonight, *(Stands and*
7   *shakes her hips)* I'm going to party till the sun comes
8   up!
9   **CINDY:** But Grandma, there's only teens here. Wouldn't you
10   rather go to a place where there's people your own age?
11   Like the Senior Citizens' Community Center? You
12   could go there and play some dominoes.
13   **GRANDMA:** Cindy, I don't want to hang out with old people!
14   **CINDY:** Me neither. *(JASON and RANDY enter.)*
15   **JASON:** Hi, Cindy.
16   **RANDY:** Hey, Cindy. Who's this?
17   **GRANDMA:** *(Offers her hand to the boys.)* Hello, boys. I'm
18   Cindy's friend.
19   **CINDY:** My friend?
20   **GRANDMA:** Just call me Patsy.
21   **RANDY:** Nice to meet you, Patsy.
22   **JASON:** Yeah, nice to meet you, Patsy.
23   **GRANDMA:** Well, I say it's time to liven up this place!
24   **CINDY:** Grandma!
25   **JASON and RANDY:** Grandma?
26   **GRANDMA:** It's just a nickname.
27   **JASON and RANDY:** Oh.
28   **LINDSEY:** *(Enters.)* Hey, guys! What's up?
29   **CINDY, JASON, and RANDY:** Hi, Lindsey.
30   **GRANDMA:** *(Offers her hand.)* Hi, I'm Cindy's friend. My
31   name's Patsy.
32   **LINDSEY:** Hi, Patsy. I'm Lindsey.
33   **GRANDMA:** And as I was saying, it's time to liven up this
34   place! Who wants to dance?
35   **CINDY:** Grandma!

1   **LINDSEY: Good idea! Come on, Jason! Let's dance!**
2   *(LINDSEY and JASON move to the side to dance.)*
3   **GRANDMA: Well, come on, Randy! Let's hit the floor!**
4   **RANDY: OK, Patsy! I'm ready!**
5   **CINDY: Grandma!**
6   **GRANDMA:** *(Turns to CINDY.)* **It's Patsy, not Grandma!** *(They*
7   *move to the side and join LINDSEY and JASON. CINDY*
8   *watches in disbelief as her grandmother does some really*
9   *wild moves.)*
10 **CINDY:** *(Trying to get her attention)* **Grandma, don't do this**
11   **to me! Go back home and knit! Go home and take your**
12   **teeth out and go to bed!** *(Looks at watch.)* **Isn't it past**
13   **your bedtime?** *(GRANDMA smiles and waves at CINDY,*
14   *then the others do, too.)* **Grandma, you're embarrassing**
15   **me!** *(After the dance, GRANDMA exits as the others join*
16   *CINDY.)*
17 **LINDSEY: Cindy, your friend's cool.**
18 **RANDY: And she's a good dancer! Did you see her out there?**
19 **CINDY: Yes, unfortunately I did.**
20 **JASON: Hey, I get the next dance with Patsy.**
21 **RANDY: Why don't you have another dance with Lindsey**
22   **first?**
23 **JASON: Because I want to dance with Patsy. It's my turn.**
24 **LINDSEY: Excuse me! Anyone want to fight over *me*?**
25 **JASON:** *(Ribs her.)* **Oh, Lindsey, you know we love you.**
26 **LINDSEY: Patsy's cool. She's fun.**
27 **CINDY:** *(Looking around)* **Uh, where did she go?**
28 **LINDSEY: Oh, she went to the Ladies Room to check her**
29   **makeup. I like the way she does her eyes, don't you?**
30 **CINDY: Lindsey, don't you think she's a little *old*?**
31 **RANDY: Who cares if she's older than us? She's cool!**
32 **JASON: Yeah, and you just remember that I get the next**
33   **dance!**
34 **CINDY: Oh, my gosh! What is wrong with all of you?**
35 **LINDSEY: What? What do you mean?**

1   **CINDY: You actually think she's cool?**

2   **LINDSEY: Yeah!**

3   **RANDY: Yeah!**

4   **JASON: She's hot, if you ask me!**

5   **CINDY: Excuse me! She can't be hot!**

6   **JASON: Why not?**

7   **CINDY: Because!**

8   **JASON: Because why?**

9   **CINDY: Because she's my *grandma*!**

10 **JASON: Oh. Well, I still want the next dance.**

11 **RANDY: Then I get the one after that.**

12 **LINDSEY: I'll be back. I'm going to ask her how she did her**

13   **eyes.** *(Exits. CINDY plops down at the table, shaking her*

14   *head in disbelief.)*

Just Act Natural

Cast (2 Male, 3 Female): Jenna, Becky, Emily, Seth, Vince
Props: Frisbees.
Setting: A park.

1 *(AT RISE: JENNA, BECKY, and EMILY are sitting on a*
2 *blanket in a park. They are staring at some girls in the*
3 *distance.)*
4 **JENNA:** I wish I was popular.
5 **BECKY:** Me, too.
6 **EMILY:** Those girls make me sick.
7 **JENNA:** Maybe if we dressed like they did for the band
8   picnic we'd be getting all the attention, too.
9 **EMILY:** Bikini tops and shorts. *(Disgusted)* **How cute.**
10 **BECKY:** My mom wouldn't let me out of the house wearing
11   stuff like that.
12 **EMILY:** Well, I wouldn't want to wear anything like that!
13 **JENNA:** Maybe it's not our clothes. Maybe it's something
14   else we're doing. Or not doing.
15 **EMILY:** Like what?
16 **JENNY:** I don't know. If I knew, we'd be more popular.
17 **BECKY:** They all think we're dorks.
18 **EMILY:** We're not dorks! We're cute! Look at us! I think
19   we're really cute! *(They look at one another.)*
20 **BECKY:** You're right.
21 **JENNY:** Yep, I think we all look pretty good.
22 **EMILY:** We're gorgeous.
23 **BECKY:** I agree.
24 **JENNY:** So, let's figure out what we're doing wrong.
25 **EMILY:** Good idea. *(Pause as they watch the other girls.)*
26 **JENNY:** I say we do what they do. You know, act like they act.
27 **BECKY:** I guess we could give it a try.

1 EMILY: Yeah, but we're missing something.

2 BECKY: What?

3 EMILY: A guy to try our stuff out on.

4 JENNA: That's true. I know. *(Hollering)* Hey, Seth! Can you
5   come over here for a minute?

6 SETH: *(Enters carrying a Frisbee.)* What?

7 JENNA: *(Acting giddy, flipping her hair from side to side, etc.)*
8   You are so good at throwing that Frisbee! We were just
9   talking about that and we wanted to tell you how
10   impressed we are!

11 SETH: OK. Well, thanks. *(Starts to leave.)*

12 BECKY: *(Quickly)* Yeah, you're the best Frisbee thrower I've
13   ever seen!

14 EMILY: Yeah, did you take lessons on how to throw a
15   Frisbee?

16 SETH: Uh ... no.

17 JENNA: Gosh, maybe sometime you could teach us how to
18   throw it like you do. Not that we'd ever be as good as
19   you.

20 SETH: Yeah, maybe. See ya. *(Exits.)*

21 EMILY: Well, that didn't go very well.

22 BECKY: Maybe because you said something stupid like,
23   "Did you take lessons on how to throw a Frisbee?"

24 EMILY: Or maybe it's because we're not wearing bikini tops
25   and short shorts!

26 JENNA: Well, something went wrong. We'll have to try
27   something else.

28 EMILY: I say it's a waste of time. We'll never get the
29   attention those girls get!

30 JENNA: Think positive. Let's try something else.

31 BECKY: OK, but what?

32 JENNA: Well, see how they're all laughing and having a
33   good time?

34 BECKY and EMILY: Yeah.

35 JENNA: Doesn't that just make you want to go over there

1   and join them?
2   BECKY and EMILY: Yeah.
3   JENNA: And look at us. What are we doing?
4   BECKY: Wishing we knew what was so funny.
5   EMILY: Wishing we were over there getting all the
6   attention.
7   JENNA: We're over here acting all depressed! So why would
8   anyone want to come over here and hang out with us?
9   BECKY: That makes sense.
10 EMILY: So we should smile and laugh and act like we're
11   having fun.
12 JENNA: Exactly!
13 BECKY: Just like they're doing.
14 JENNA: Yeah.
15 EMILY: Well, I guess we can fake it and act stupid like them.
16 BECKY: But if it works, maybe we'll go from pretending to
17   have fun to actually having fun.
18 JENNA: That's the right attitude, Becky! This is going to
19   work! I just know it!
20 EMILY: I hope so.
21 JENNA: OK, on the count of three, we'll start. One, two,
22   three ... *(They begin laughing, acting silly and throwing a*
23   *nearby Frisbee.)*
24 BECKY: Throw it to me!
25 EMILY: *(Laughing)* I'm not very good, but I'll try!
26 BECKY: *(Glancing off)* No one's noticing.
27 JENNA: Keep laughing. Don't stop. Just give it some time to
28   work.
29 BECKY: *(Laughing)* I feel really stupid!
30 EMILY: *(Laughing)* Me, too!
31 BECKY: And we probably look stupid, too!
32 JENNA: Don't look now, but Seth and Vince are headed this
33   way!
34 BECKY: *(Laughing)* Maybe it's working!
35 EMILY: *(Laughing)* This is great!

1 JENNA: OK, just act natural.

2 BECKY: *(Laughing)* **This isn't natural.**

3 EMILY: *(Laughing)* **Yeah, and if we act natural, no one will**
4   **give us any attention.**

5 JENNA: **I know, let's act like we could care less that Seth and**
6   **Vince come over.**

7 EMILY: **Good idea.** *(They continue to laugh and throw the*
8   *Frisbee. SETH and VINCE enter.)*

9 VINCE: **Hey.**

10 JENNA: **Hey.** *(To EMILY)* **Throw it to me, Emily.** *(The girls*
11   *laugh and toss the Frisbee, completely ignoring the boys.)*

12 SETH: **Uh ... excuse us.**

13 BECKY: **That was a great catch! Now, throw it back to me!**

14 EMILY: **OK, get ready!**

15 VINCE: **Uh ... could we borrow your Frisbee?** *(The girls*
16   *immediately stop laughing and look at the boys,*
17   *obviously disappointed.)*

18 JENNA: **What?**

19 BECKY: **You want to borrow our Frisbee?**

20 EMILY: **In case you didn't notice, we were having fun!**

21 SETH: **Look, it's obvious ...**

22 JENNA: **It's obvious?**

23 SETH: **It's obvious that you girls don't know how to throw a**
24   **Frisbee, and we need another one because ours got**
25   **stuck in the tree.**

26 JENNA: **So you don't want to stay here and throw it with us?**

27 SETH: **No!**

28 VINCE: **Come on; let us borrow your Frisbee.**

29 JENNA: *(Tightly holding onto it)* **No!**

30 VINCE: **Fine. Come on, Seth.** *(The boys exit.)*

31 BECKY: **So much for that idea!**

32 EMILY: **Guess we don't have what it takes to be popular.**

33 JENNA: **Well, who would want to be!**

34 BECKY: **Uh, we did, remember?**

35 JENNA: **It's not worth it if we have to act stupid!**

1   EMILY: That was stupid.

2   BECKY: Well, let's look at the bright side.

3   EMILY: What bright side?

4   BECKY: Well, we're popular amongst ourselves!

5   JENNA: That's true. So forget about all that stuff and let's just

6   be ourselves and have fun.

7   EMILY: That's what I say!

8   BECKY: Me, too! *(They begin laughing and tossing the Frisbee.)*

9   EMILY: You know, this is more fun when we're not trying to

10   impress people.

11 BECKY: Yeah, forget them!

12 JENNA: Who cares what they think! At least we know we're

13   fun to be around.

14 EMILY: And don't forget that we're cute!

15 BECKY: And popular! At least amongst ourselves.

16 EMILY: We're popular in our own way!

17 JENNA: Look! Seth and Vince are coming back over here.

18 BECKY: Big deal.

19 EMILY: They probably just want to ask for the Frisbee again.

20 JENNA: And they're *not* getting it! *(SETH and VINCE enter.)*

21 VINCE: Hey.

22 GIRLS: Hey.

23 SETH: Uh ... Can we join in? *(The girls look at each other.)*

24 JENNA: *(A bit rude)* Why? So you can steal our Frisbee?

25 SETH: No. It just looked like you were having fun and we

26   thought we'd come back over.

27 VINCE: Yeah, everyone else over there is fighting over the

28   Frisbee.

29 SETH: So it looked like more fun over here. Hey, Jenna, you

30   want me to show you how to throw that Frisbee?

31 JENNA: Sure! *(SETH stands behind JENNA and instructs her on*

32   *holding the Frisbee as the others watch. They are all*

33   *laughing and having a good time.)*

The Umbrella

Cast (2 Male, 3 Female): Brad, Marla, Alice, Todd, Cassie
Props: Umbrella, newspaper, purse.
Setting: Outside an ice cream shop on a rainy day.

1   *(AT RISE: BRAD enters carrying a newspaper and an*
2   *umbrella. He is looking up at the sky as MARLA enters.)*
3   **MARLA:** Oh, are they not open yet?
4   **BRAD:** Not yet.
5   **MARLA:** Oh. Well, I'm here to apply for the job, what about
6   you?
7   **BRAD:** Same here. Guess we're in competition.
8   **MARLA:** Maybe they're going to hire more than one person.
9   **BRAD:** *(Looking at the paper)* More than one assistant
10   manager?
11   **MARLA:** Maybe. Do you have experience?
12   **BRAD:** Scooping ice cream? Well, last summer I worked at
13   The Penguin. You know, that snow cone hut?
14   **MARLA:** Well, that's good experience.
15   **BRAD:** What about you?
16   **MARLA:** I spent all last summer babysitting. But now that I
17   have my own car, I'm ready to venture out into the real
18   world. Besides, my parents are forcing me to get a job.
19   You know, gas money, insurance, et cetera, et cetera.
20   **BRAD:** I can relate.
21   **MARLA:** *(Looking up)* So, do you think it's going to rain?
22   **BRAD:** Looks pretty dark. I wouldn't be surprised.
23   **MARLA:** My luck. Off without my umbrella.
24   **BRAD:** You could always sit in your car.
25   **MARLA:** My car's in the shop. My mom dropped me off.
26   **BRAD:** I took the city bus.
27   **MARLA:** *(Looking at her watch)* I wonder why they haven't

1   opened up yet?

2 BRAD: I think we're early. I was hoping to be the first one

3   here so I'd have a better chance at getting the job.

4 MARLA: That was smart. Well, if they do hire two

5   assistants, then at least I'll be next in line. Oh no! I just

6   felt a sprinkle.

7 BRAD: Me, too. *(Smiles, opens umbrella.)*

8 MARLA: And another, and another, and another! Oh, my

9   hair! I'm going to be a mess.

10 BRAD: Ah, I love the smell of rain. *(He takes a deep breath*

11   *and continues to smile as he stands under the umbrella.)*

12 MARLA: Look, do you think I could stand under the

13   umbrella with you? Please!

14 BRAD: Sure.

15 MARLA: Oh, thank you! *(Rushes underneath the umbrella.)*

16   You're a lifesaver! My hair doesn't do well in rain. It

17   gets all frizzy, and I want to make a good impression

18   when they interview me for the job.

19 BRAD: *(Offers his hand.)* I'm Brad.

20 MARLA: *(Shakes his hand.)* I'm Marla. Nice to meet you,

21   Brad.

22 ALICE: *(Enters.)* They're not open?

23 BRAD: Nope.

24 MARLA: Not yet.

25 ALICE: *(Looks at the sky.)* Of all the days! And this is a dry-

26   clean-only outfit!

27 MARLA: It's nice.

28 BRAD: Nice color.

29 ALICE: Oh, and these spots that you see are not a part of the

30   material! Oh! This rain is ruining my new outfit!

31 MARLA: Why don't you squeeze in here with us?

32 ALICE: Oh, do you mind?

33 BRAD: *(Looking at Marla)* Uh ...

34 MARLA: No, not at all! Come on! Hurry! *(The girls stand*

35   *together in the front, pushing BRAD to the back.)*

1   ALICE: Oh, thank you! I'm Alice.

2   MARLA: I'm Marla.

3   BRAD: *(Pokes his head out.)* **I'm Brad.**

4   ALICE: So, are you both here to apply for the job?

5   MARLA: Yes.

6   BRAD: *(Pokes his head out.)* **Yes!**

7   ALICE: I wonder how many people they're going to hire?

8   MARLA: Brad thinks they'll only hire one assistant
9   manager.

10 ALICE: Who's Brad?

11 BRAD: *(Pokes his head out.)* **Me! Brad with the umbrella!**

12 MARLA: But I was hoping they'd hire more than one, you
13   know, for different shifts.

14 ALICE: Maybe.

15 TODD: *(Enters.)* **Man, oh man, oh man! First I have car**
16   **problems, then I get grease on my sleeves, and now it**
17   **has to rain!** *(Notices the others standing under the*
18   *umbrella.)* **Oh, hi.**

19 ALICE: Hi.

20 MARLA: Hi.

21 BRAD: *(Pokes his head out.)* **Hi.**

22 TODD: **And I should've brought my umbrella!** *(They all*
23   *nod.)* **I'm here to apply for the job. I guess y'all are, too,**
24   **huh?**

25 ALICE: I am.

26 MARLA: Me, too.

27 BRAD: *(Pokes his head out.)* **I was here first!**

28 TODD: **Yeah, and I'm going to be greasy and soaked! That**
29   **ought to impress the manager! Man, it's really starting**
30   **to come down! Hey, do you think I could find a tiny spot**
31   **to stick my head under your umbrella?**

32 ALICE: Sure you can! Come on!

33 MARLA: I think there's room

34 BRAD: *(Pokes his head out.)* **I don't think there's enough**
35   **room here!**

1 TODD: Thanks, girls. *(As he gets under the umbrella, it*
2   *pushes BRAD even further back.)*
3 CASSIE: *(Enters.)* **What, they're not open?** *(Others shake*
4   *heads.)* **Oh, great!** *(Puts her purse over her head.)* **This is**
5   **just great! Oh, I should've brought my umbrella!**
6   *(Others nod heads.)* **My face is going to be a mess! I'll**
7   **probably have mascara running down my face! And**
8   **won't that look nice! Gosh, do you think there's room**
9   **for one more?**
10 TODD: **You bet, sweetheart! Come stand over here by me!**
11 ALICE: **Well, I don't know ...**
12 MARLA: **It's already pretty crowded!**
13 BRAD: *(Pokes head out.)* **I'm getting wet back here!**
14 CASSIE: **Oh, thank you!** *(Stands by TODD.)* **I'm Cassie.**
15 TODD: **Nice to meet you Cassie. I'm Todd.**
16 ALICE: **Alice, here.**
17 MARLA: **I'm Marla.**
18 BRAD: *(Pokes his head out.)* **I'm Brad, and this is my**
19   **umbrella!**
20 CASSIE: **Wow, it's really starting to rain!**
21 ALICE: **Can you move over? I need some more room!**
22 MARLA: **I can't move. If I do, my hair will get wet and start**
23   **to frizz.**
24 ALICE: **And what about my outfit? Remember, this is a dry-**
25   **clean-only outfit!**
26 MARLA: **Well, I'm sorry, but I was here before you!**
27 TODD: **Hey, quit pushing!**
28 CASSIE: **Can I scoot in just a tiny bit more, please?**
29 MARLA: **Hey, you're pushing me out!**
30 TODD: **No, you're pushing everyone else out!**
31 MARLA: **I am not!**
32 ALICE: **Yes you are!**
33 BRAD: *(Pokes his head out.)* **I'm getting wet back here!**
34 TODD: **Can't you girls be nice and share?**
35 CASSIE: **I need more room! I don't want my mascara to run!**

1 MARLA: Excuse me, but I'm the one who's sharing here,
2   and I'm getting all wet!
3 ALICE: Move over!
4 MARLA: *You* move over!
5 CASSIE: Hey, I need more room!
6 TODD: Quit pushing!
7 MARLA: You don't have to be such a hog!
8 ALICE: Me? You're the one who's the hog!
9 CASSIE: Can't I please have some more room?
10 TODD: Ouch! Someone stepped on my foot!
11 BRAD: *(Pokes his head out.)* I'm getting wet back here!
12 ALICE: I need to get under the umbrella just a little bit
13   more so my outfit doesn't get ruined!
14 MARLA: And I'm worried about my hair! I don't want it to
15   frizz!
16 CASSIE: Excuse me! This makeup is not waterproof!
17 TODD: Look, I'm hardly under the umbrella. Can't you
18   girls give me a little more room here?
19 MARLA: Quit pushing!
20 ALICE: You quit pushing!
21 CASSIE: Move back!
22 MARLA: You move!
23 ALICE: No, you move!
24 TODD: Stop pushing! Stop it!
25 BRAD: *(Jumping up and down, poking his head out.)* Excuse
26   me! Can I have my umbrella back?
27 CASSIE: Scoot over!
28 MARLA: I was here first!
29 CASSIE: So? You can still share!
30 MARLA: I am sharing!
31 ALICE: Move over!
32 TODD: You move over! *(BRAD walks out from behind the*
33   *umbrella and stands in front of them. A pause.)*
34 CASSIE: Who's he?
35 BRAD: I'm Brad and this is *my umbrella*!

1   **CASSIE: Oh.**

2   **MARLA: Will you please move over?**

3   **ALICE: I did move over!**

4   **TODD: Hey, stop pushing!**

5   **CASSIE: Stop! You're pushing me out!**

6   **MARLA: Move over!**

7   **ALICE: You move over!** *(As they continue to fight, BRAD*

8   *shakes his head and walks away.)*

Take Your Kid to Work Day

Cast (4 Male, 1 Female): Dr. Foster, Ryan,
Janet, John, Doug
Props: Desk, chairs, briefcase, day planner.
Setting: A therapist's office waiting room.

1   *(AT RISE: DR. FOSTER and RYAN enter an office. DR.*
2   *FOSTER carries a briefcase.)*
3   **DR. FOSTER:** I love this tradition our city celebrates — Take
4   Your Kid to Work Day.
5   **RYAN:** Me, too! Anything to get out of school!
6   **DR. FOSTER:** Now look, Ryan, my job's not as easy as it seems.
7   And I think you'll gain some respect for your dad when
8   you see what I actually have to put up with every day.
9   **RYAN:** Come on, Dad, your job is a cinch! Gosh, all you have to
10   do is sit around and listen to people gripe about their
11   problems. How hard can that be?
12   **DR. FOSTER:** Well, son, it's not as easy as it sounds.
13   **RYAN:** Yeah, I know, I know. You have to jump in there from
14   time to time and offer your clients some advice. But hey,
15   for a hundred dollars an hour, I could handle that!
16   **DR. FOSTER:** I'm telling you; it's not as easy as it sounds.
17   **RYAN:** Sure, sure.
18   **DR. FOSTER:** I've given Paula, my secretary, the day off since
19   you'll be here to me help out.
20   **RYAN:** Cool.
21   **DR. FOSTER:** *(Looks at his watch.)* And as usual, things never
22   go as planned. I need to run to the courthouse for
23   mediation. It shouldn't take too long, but just in case, do
24   you think you can handle things here while I'm gone?

1 RYAN: Sure, no problem.
2 DR. FOSTER: Now listen, I have three appointments set for
3   this morning, so I need you to explain to my clients that
4   I'm running a bit late. Assure them that I'll be back and
5   we'll still have our session.
6 RYAN: Relax, Dad, I've got you covered.
7 DR. FOSTER: All right. I'll be back as soon as I can.
8 RYAN: Take your time. Don't rush. I can handle things here.
9   *(DR. FOSTER exits, and RYAN sits down at the desk.)* Man,
10   for a hundred bucks an hour, I could handle this! Beats
11   sitting in algebra class! Hmmm ... Maybe dad will see what
12   a good job I've done and hire me as his partner. Foster and
13   Foster. Yeah! Foster and Foster Counseling Center. Yeah, I
14   like that!
15 JANET: *(Entering)* Uh, hello. I'm here for my appointment with
16   Dr. Foster.
17 RYAN: Oh, well my dad, I mean, Dr. Foster had to step out of
18   the office, but he'll be back soon. So, just, uh ... have a seat!
19 JANET: I'd rather stand, thank you. *(Pointing to a chair)* Did you
20   know there are over a million germs on that chair?
21 RYAN: Well, at least you can't see them!
22 JANET: But they're still there. I don't like germs.
23 RYAN: Just pretend they're not there.
24 JANET: Do you know what I'm afraid of more than germs?
25 RYAN: No, what?
26 JANET: Death!
27 RYAN: That's stupid.
28 JANET: Stupid?
29 RYAN: Yeah! Everyone's going to die, so why waste your time
30   worrying about it?
31 JANET: Because dying scares me!
32 RYAN: *(Laughs.)* Well, you won't be scared when you're dead!
33 JANET: How do you know?
34 RYAN: Because you'll be dead! Duh!
35 JANET: When is Dr. Foster coming back? Because I really need

1   **to talk to him!** *(Pointing to the floor)* **What's that?**

2   **RYAN: Uh ... it looks like a piece of fuzz.**

3   **JANET: No it's not! I think it's a bug!**

4   **RYAN:** *(Stomps on the floor, then picks something up.)* **Look, it was**

5   **just a piece of fuzz.** *(Laughing)* **I just killed a piece of fuzz.**

6   **JANET: Don't say that word!**

7   **RYAN: What word?**

8   **JANET: You know what word!**

9   **RYAN: Fuzz?**

10   **JANET: No, the other word!**

11   **RYAN: Killed?**

12   **JANET: I said don't say that word! Because you know what**

13   **happens if that happens.**

14   **RYAN: I think I'm a little confused here.**

15   **JANET: If that word happens, you die!**

16   **RYAN: OK.**

17   **JANET: And I'm afraid of death, remember?**

18   **RYAN: Well, just relax. Look, it's not a bug; it's just a tiny piece of**

19   **fuzz.**

20   **JANET: Did you know there are over ten thousand germs on that**

21   **piece of fuzz?**

22   **RYAN:** *(Looking at it)* **Cool! I wish I had a microscope so I could**

23   **see them!**

24   **JANET: Get it away from me!**

25   **RYAN: Gosh, you're afraid of everything, aren't you?**

26   **JANET: No, just germs, insects, and death!**

27   **RYAN: And fuzz! Gosh, just calm down. Take a chill pill. This**

28   **little piece of fuzz isn't going to kill you. You know, maybe**

29   **you should face your fears. That's what my dad always**

30   **taught me.** *(Holding out the fuzz)* **Go ahead. Touch it. Better**

31   **yet, put it in your mouth and swallow it! That's the way to**

32   **face your fears!**

33   **JANET:** *No! No! Get it away from me!*

34   **RYAN: Look, this itty bitty piece of fuzz won't hurt you. Look! It's**

35   **not hurting me.**

1 JANET: *Go away!* That piece of fuzz has *thousands* of germs on it!

2 RYAN: So? Who cares? *(Holding it in front of her mouth)* Eat it!

3   Come on! You can do it!

4 JANET: *No! No! No!*

5 RYAN: OK, OK, OK! I'll throw it away. *(Takes it to the trash can,*

6   *then sits down at the desk.)* Man! It was just a little piece of

7   fuzz!

8 JOHN: *(Entering)* Hello. I have an appointment with Dr. Foster.

9 RYAN: Dr. Foster stepped out for a moment, but he'll be back

10   soon.

11 JOHN: This is not good! I have a schedule to follow! *(Opens*

12   *planner.)* This will ruin my entire day! *(Looks at Janet.)* Is

13   she before me?

14 RYAN: Yes.

15 JOHN: *(To Janet)* Do you mind if I cut? I have a very tight

16   schedule.

17 JANET: Well, so do I! Besides, I don't want to be in this germ-

18   infested office any longer than I have to!

19 RYAN: Sir, why don't you have a seat?

20 JOHN: *(Straightens chair before sitting.)* Thank you.

21 JANET: *(To JOHN)* Did you know there are over a million germs

22   on that chair?

23 JOHN: *(Ignoring her)* All these chairs are crooked. *(Gets up and*

24   *begins straightening all the chairs.)*

25 JANET: I wouldn't touch all those if I were you!

26 RYAN: Sir ...

27 JOHN: John! My name's John Baxter!

28 RYAN: Uh, Mr. Baxter, I wouldn't worry about those chairs. I'm

29   sure the cleaning lady will ...

30 JOHN: Can't relax if things are out of order!

31 JANET: *(Reaches into her purse.)* Do you want to borrow some

32   of my hand cleaner? It kills ninety-nine point nine percent

33   of the germs on your hands. *(Uses some herself.)*

34 JOHN: Nope. *(Goes to Ryan.)* Want me to tidy up your desk?

35 RYAN: No, that's OK. But thanks.

1   JOHN: *(Sits down. To JANET)* **Don't you want to sit down? The**
2   **chairs are nice and straight now.** *(JANET shakes her head.)*
3   **OK.** *(Jumps up.)* **Do you have any glass cleaner? That**
4   **mirror has streaks.**
5   RYAN: Look, I think my dad, I mean, Dr. Foster ... has a
6   cleaning lady, so don't worry about it.
7   JOHN: But I don't mind! You see, it's just hard for me to relax
8   when things are dirty.
9   RYAN: Man, then you'd die if you saw my room!
10 JANET: *Die?* Don't say that word! I hate that word!
11 JOHN: What? Die?
12 JANET: Yes, I hate that word! Don't say it! *(DOUG enters.)*
13 RYAN: May I help you?
14 DOUG: Not unless you're Dr. Foster!
15 RYAN: I'm not, I'm ...
16 DOUG: I know you're not Dr. Foster! Don't you think I know
17   that! So, where is he?
18 RYAN: He's not here, but ...
19 DOUG: Not here? What do you mean he's not here?
20 RYAN: He had to step out for a minute, but he'll be back soon.
21 DOUG: Man, this is unacceptable! I'm here on time, so he
22   should be here on time!
23 RYAN: Why don't you just have a seat and relax. It shouldn't be
24   much longer. *(Angrily, DOUG plops down in a chair.)*
25 JOHN: Hey, I just straightened up that chair!
26 JANET: Did you know there are over one million germs on that
27   chair?
28 DOUG: You know, this really makes me mad! I didn't come
29   here to sit around and waste my time!
30 RYAN: Sir, Dr. Foster will be back as soon as possible. Please
31   just calm down.
32 DOUG: Kid, if I could calm down I wouldn't come here for
33   counseling!
34 RYAN: Well, there's nothing to get so upset about.
35 DOUG: Nothing to get upset about?! How about being stuck in

1   this office with a bunch of wackos?

2 JOHN: Hey, everyone's got problems!

3 JANET: I don't have problems. I'm just afraid of dying.

4 JOHN: And I may be a little obsessive, but it's better than

5   someone who can't control his anger! Especially for no

6   reason!

7 DOUG: Hey, I've got my reasons!

8 JOHN: Yeah? Name one?

9 DOUG: You! How's that for a reason?

10 RYAN: OK, OK, let's just all sit down and relax. My dad, I mean,

11   Dr. Foster, will be here very soon.

12 JANET: I'm not sitting down! Did you know there are over a

13   million germs ...

14 ALL: *Yes!*

15 DOUG: And I don't like being told what to do! So, no, I don't

16   think I'll sit down! I think I'll stand!

17 JOHN: Do y'all ever vacuum this place? Man! *(Gets on his hands*

18   *and knees and starts cleaning.)* There's fuzzies all over the

19   floor.

20 JANET: *(Beginning to panic, she watches every step she takes.)*

21   There are?

22 JOHN: And here's a spider! *(Hits it with his hand.)* Got it! It's

23   dead now!

24 JANET: Dead? *Dead?*

25 JOHN: Yep, it's dead. Wanna see?

26 JANET: *Dead?*

27 JOHN: I thought you didn't like bugs.

28 JANET: I don't, but I didn't want it dead! What if it had a

29   family? You know, a spider family? Kids? You know, kid

30   spiders? What if it was on its way to feed its children?

31 JOHN: Its children?

32 DOUG: Lady, are you crazy?

33 JANET: And you've just ended an innocent spider's life!

34 JOHN: And to the trash can we go! *(To RYAN)* Do you want me

35   to take out the trash?

1   JANET: We should say a prayer.

2   DOUG: What, pray for a stupid spider? Lady, you're nuts!

3   JANET: And you are very mean!

4   JOHN: *(To RYAN)* Do you know where the vacuum cleaner is?

5   DOUG: You're both nuts!

6   JOHN: These fuzzies on the floor are driving me crazy!

7   DOUG: I'll second that!

8   JANET: Do you know how many germs are on each piece of
9   fuzz?

10 DOUG: We don't care, lady! Understand? We don't care!

11 JOHN: Well, I'm going to pick them up! Even if it takes me all
12   day! *(Sits on floor.)* Of course, this is going to mess up my
13   entire schedule for the day. Oh well. What's more
14   important is a clean office. *(Picking up fuzzies)* Because I
15   can't stand a mess!

16 DOUG: You guys are sick!

17 JANET: Sick? Sick? If we're sick, that means we're going to ...
18   to ...

19 DOUG: Die?

20 JANET: Don't say that word!

21 DOUG: What word? Die? *Die, die, die!*

22 JANET: *(Covers her ears.)* *Stop it!*

23 JOHN: *(To DOUG)* Would you move your foot? I need to clean
24   right there.

25 JANET: I hate that word, I hate that word, I hate that word ...

26 JOHN: Move your foot!

27 DOUG: Hey, why don't you make me?

28 JANET: It's true. Death scares me. I admit that. Because when
29   you die ... you're ... you're ... *dead!*

30 DOUG: Well, duh! It doesn't take much to figure that out!

31 RYAN: Uh ... if you could just all sit down and relax. Dr. Foster
32   will be here soon. So let's all just sit down, OK?

33 JANET: I'm not sitting down!

34 JOHN: And I'm busy cleaning the floor. Would you *please*
35   move your foot?

1 **DOUG: Does it look like I'm going to move my foot?**

2 **JANET: Because when you're dead, you can't do anything fun**

3 **ever again.**

4 **DOUG: Well, why don't you try to have some fun before you die**

5 **instead of making everyone miserable?**

6 **JOHN: OK, I'll just come back to this area, thank you very**

7 **much!** *(DR. FOSTER enters and everyone freezes.)*

8 **DR. FOSTER: I'm back! Everything OK around here?** *(They ALL*

9 *smile and nod their heads.)*

King and Queen

Cast (2 Male, 3 Female): Jerry, Leann, Kip, Ashley, Mrs. Waters

1 JERRY: Leann, I know you hate my guts, but can't you fake it for
2   an hour or so?

3 LEANN: *(Turns away, crossing her arms.)* No!

4 JERRY: You know, you're going to make me look bad.

5 LEANN: I don't care!

6 JERRY: Leann, don't you think it *might* be fun? I mean, how
7   many times are you named King and Queen of your school?
8   And we are, like it or not, one of the main attractions of the
9   parade!

10 LEANN: I'd rather wash my hair.

11 JERRY: Think about it, Leann! The school band will lead the way
12   as we sit on top of that float. Our crowns firmly in place ...
13   *(Smiling and waving)* We'll smile and wave to the crowd ...

14 LEANN: You can smile and wave to the crowd.

15 JERRY: And for one night, we're celebrities! The King and Queen
16   of Bowie High! You know, it doesn't get much better than
17   that!

18 LEANN: It'd be better if I weren't forced to sit next to you!

19 JERRY: Well, fine, then! Be that way! Frown, cross your arms,
20   refuse to wave! But not me! I'm going to look great! *(Smiles*
21   *and waves.)* I'm going to smile and wave ... while you just sit
22   there and sulk and look miserable. Won't that look cute? You
23   know my friend Ted? Well, he's going to capture us on my
24   video camera. That'll be fun to show to all my friends and
25   family! What a laugh! The King and *Grouch* of Bowie High!

26 LEANN: Shut up! Will you just shut up! And please don't sit too
27   close to me or I might just throw up!

28 JERRY: Well, if you do, throw up on yourself! Or I know! Lean

1   over the float and puke to the side as we're going down
2   Main Street. Man, Ted's gonna get this on video for me!
3 LEANN: Well, how about if I *accidentally* push you off the
4   float? Oops! See ya! Goodbye!
5 JERRY: *(Laughs.)* You wish!
6 LEANN: Oh, this is going to be miserable! Finally, my dream
7   comes true and it's ruined because of you!
8 JERRY: Well, obviously the students of Bowie High don't feel
9   the same way towards me as you do. *(Smiling proudly)*
10   They all like me. I was voted King! And by the way, why do
11   you hate me?
12 LEANN: Jerry, don't ask me such a stupid question. I've hated
13   you since second grade!
14 JERRY: I know, but why?
15 LEANN: I don't want to talk about this.
16 JERRY: Well, I do! For once I'd like to know why you hate me ...
17   since second grade!
18 LEANN: Just drop it! *(KIP and ASHLEY enter.)*
19 KIP: The Prince and Princess have arrived!
20 ASHLEY: And we'll be right behind you in the parade. Oh,
21   Leann, you look so pretty.
22 LEANN: Thanks.
23 ASHLEY: I'm so excited! I can't wait until it begins!
24 LEANN: And it's perfect since you and Kip have been going out
25   for three months.
26 KIP: Two people who not only found love, but fame as well.
27   Ashley, sweetheart, we are one hot couple!
28 JERRY: Yeah, well, it's too bad Queen Leann here hates my
29   guts! We'll probably be arguing during the entire parade.
30   I'll be saying, "Smile, wave ... come on, smile and wave!"
31   And Queen Leann will be screaming, "Don't talk to me,
32   you moron! Why are you sitting so close? Don't touch me!
33   I hate you!"
34 ASHLEY: Leann, just try to fake it. Pretend he's not there.
35 KIP: So Leann, why do you hate Jerry so much?

1   JERRY: She's hated me since second grade.

2   ASHLEY: Gosh Jerry, what did you do? Steal her crayons? *(They*

3   *all laugh except for LEANN.)*

4   KIP: Pull her hair? *(They laugh.)*

5   ASHLEY: Chase her around the playground and make her fall

6   down and skin her knee?

7   JERRY: Actually, I don't remember.

8   LEANN: Oh, yes you do!

9   JERRY: No I don't!

10 LEANN: Yes you do!

11 MRS. WATERS: *(Entering)* All right, we'll be starting soon. Now

12   remember to wave and smile.

13 JERRY: *(Nudges LEANN.)* Yeah, remember to wave and smile.

14 MRS. WATERS: The small children really look up to you, and

15   they get so excited. You remember how it was when you

16   were a kid.

17 JERRY: I wish I did.

18 LEANN: You do, but you just refuse to admit it!

19 JERRY: I do not!

20 LEANN: Do too!

21 MRS. WATERS: Are we having a little problem over here?

22 JERRY: No, Mrs. Waters. I was just trying to remember what it

23   was like to be a kid. For some reason I just can't recall, but

24   Leann thinks I'm lying, but I'm not, and I was just trying

25   to explain ...

26 MRS. WATERS: All right, all right, enough of that. Let's all get

27   ready to take our places. And remember, wave and smile!

28   *(She exits.)*

29 KIP: Come on my beautiful princess, let's go.

30 ASHLEY: See you two after the parade. Remember there's a

31   dance in the gym afterwards.

32 JERRY: We'll be there. Well not together, but we'll be there.

33   *(KIP and ASHLEY exit.)*

34 LEANN: OK, let's get this over with.

35 JERRY: Will you try to smile? Please!

1   LEANN: Why don't you worry about yourself and not about
2   me!
3   JERRY: Oh, my gosh! Will you *please* tell me what I did to you
4   in second grade!
5   LEANN: All right, fine, Mr. Liar who *pretends* he can't
6   remember! Yes, you did chase me on the playground!
7   JERRY: OK, well I'm sorry! I don't remember, but I'm really
8   truly sorry. So, can you just get over it and forgive and
9   forget? *Please?*
10 LEANN: Do you know what chasing a girl on the playground
11   means?
12 JERRY: Well ... yeah. It meant that I liked you.
13 LEANN: Exactly!
14 JERRY: OK, well I'm sorry for liking you in second grade?
15 LEANN: You led me on, made me think that you liked me, and
16   then ... then ...
17 JERRY: Then what?
18 LEANN: Then you broke my heart, that's what!
19 JERRY: I broke your heart?
20 LEANN: Remember? I passed you that note with the hearts all
21   over it!
22 JERRY: Uh ...
23 LEANN: And it said, "Will you go out with me?"
24 JERRY: Oh yeah! Now I remember!
25 LEANN: And what did you do?
26 JERRY: Well, this is a little embarrassing for me. I read your
27   note, and I cried.
28 LEANN: I know! Talk about making a girl feel bad! And *that's*
29   why I hate you!
30 JERRY: Leann, I cried because I was scared of girls, not
31   because I didn't like you.
32 LEANN: You weren't scared of girls! You chased me all over the
33   playground!
34 JERRY: Yeah, but you always ran away from me. That was safe
35   for me.

1 LEANN: You mean ...

2 JERRY: Yes I liked you! I've always liked you! And I still like

3   you. Except when you're mean to me, which is most of the

4   time, but besides that, I like you.

5 LEANN: Really?

6 JERRY: Really!

7 LEANN: Wow. And to think I've hated you since second grade

8   for not liking me when you really did like me. You know,

9   this just turns my childhood completely upside down. It's

10   like I've been living a lie!

11 JERRY: Me not liking you is definitely a lie. Why, I'd go out with

12   you today if you'd pass me another note.

13 LEANN: You would?

14 JERRY: Yes.

15 LEANN: Really?

16 JERRY: Yes! *(Holds out his hand for hers.)* Come on, my Queen,

17   we've got a parade to attend.

18 LEANN: *(Takes his hand.)* And I'll be waving and smiling the

19   entire time.

20 JERRY: *(Kisses her cheek.)* Me, too.

Condiments

Cast (3 Male, 2 Female): Meagan, Amber, Chris,
John, Robbie
Props: Two salt shakers, two pepper shakers,
three bottles of ketchup.
Setting: School cafeteria.

1   *(AT RISE: MEAGAN and AMBER are sitting at one table*
2   *while CHRIS, JOHN, and ROBBIE are at another table.)*
3   **MEAGAN:** *(After looking at the boys)* **Amber, you've got to help**
4   **me get his attention!**
5   **AMBER: Meagan, don't act like we're in junior high. Just walk**
6   **over to his table and say hi!**
7   **MEAGAN: Are you kidding? Just walk over and say hi?**
8   **AMBER: Sure.**
9   **MEAGAN: And then what? Crawl under the table when he**
10   **looks at me like I'm weird or something?**
11   **AMBER: Wait and see what he says.**
12   **MEAGAN: Well, you want to hook up with Chris, so why don't**
13   **you walk over there and just say hi? If it works, then I'll**
14   **take your advice.**
15   **AMBER: OK.** *(Goes to the boys' table.)* **Hi.**
16   **CHRIS: Hi.** *(Pause)* **What? Do you need to borrow the salt or**
17   **something?**
18   **AMBER: Uh, yeah. Thanks.** *(Takes the salt and leaves.)*
19   **JOHN: Hey, Chris, I think she likes you.**
20   **ROBBIE: Hey, I thought she was looking at me.**
21   **CHRIS: Whatever.**
22   **MEAGAN: Well? How'd it go?**
23   **AMBER: Great!**
24   **MEAGAN: What'd he say?**
25   **AMBER: He said hi.**

1   **MEAGAN:** And?

2   **AMBER:** And ... "Do you need to borrow the salt or something?"

3   **MEAGAN:** *(Laughs.)* **Oh, that went well!**

4   **AMBER:** It's a start. Now he knows who I am.

5   **MEAGAN:** It's embarrassing if you ask me!

6   **AMBER:** OK, it's your turn. Go over and introduce yourself to

7   John. I know, ask to borrow the pepper.

8   **MEAGAN:** But that is so obvious!

9   **AMBER:** But it's a good way to meet him. Come on, Meagan!

10   You promised to do it if I did.

11   **MEAGAN:** *(Reluctantly, she stands.)* **OK.** *(Goes to the table. To*

12   *John)* **Hi.**

13   **JOHN:** Hi.

14   **MEAGAN:** Uh ... could I borrow the pepper?

15   **JOHN:** Sure, no problem.

16   **MEAGAN:** Thanks. *(Takes the pepper and leaves.)*

17   **CHRIS:** Hey, John, I think she likes you.

18   **ROBBIE:** No, I think it's me she's after.

19   **JOHN:** Whatever.

20   **AMBER:** Well, what did he say?

21   **MEAGAN:** He said, "Sure, no problem."

22   **AMBER:** Hey, it's a start.

23   **MEAGAN:** It was stupid!

24   **CHRIS:** *(Goes to the girls' table.)* **Can I have the salt back?**

25   **AMBER:** Sure. I'm sorry I didn't return it.

26   **CHRIS:** No problem. *(He leaves.)*

27   **AMBER:** See, it did work! Chris came over and started up a

28   conversation with me! Yes, I believe we're on our way to a

29   long-lasting relationship!

30   **MEAGAN:** I hardly think that him asking for the salt back is

31   the beginning of true love.

32   **AMBER:** Oh, you are so negative.

33   **MEAGAN:** Amber, he just needed the salt. Gosh, you are so

34   stupid sometimes!

35   **JOHN:** *(Goes to the girls' table.)* **Uh ... could I borrow the pepper?**

1   MEAGAN: Sure! Here you go.

2   JOHN: Thanks. *(Leaves.)*

3   MEAGAN: Oh, my gosh! Did you see that? He looked right at me

4   and asked for the pepper! And for a second, when I

5   handed him the pepper, our thumbs touched! Oh, I'm in

6   love!

7   AMBER: I thought you said my idea was stupid.

8   MEAGAN: Well, I'm sorry. It was a good idea. But now what? I

9   mean, do we go over there and ask to borrow the salt and

10   pepper again? Or do we just sit here and wait?

11   AMBER: We ignore them.

12   MEAGAN: What?

13   AMBER: We ignore them. Now they know we're interested in

14   them, so now it's time to play hard to get.

15   MEAGAN: I don't want to play hard to get! I know – what if we

16   go over there and ask to borrow the ketchup?

17   AMBER: No, that's too obvious. We just have to wait. And it'd

18   help if we laughed so they wouldn't think we were just

19   sitting here waiting on them to come back over.

20   MEAGAN: I guess.

21   AMBER: So, let's start laughing. *(They talk quietly, then burst*

22   *out laughing from time to time.)*

23   ROBBIE: Which one do y'all like? The salt or the pepper?

24   CHRIS: The salt.

25   JOHN: The pepper.

26   ROBBIE: Actually, I like the salt and pepper. Decisions,

27   decisions ...

28   JOHN: You think they were trying to get our attention?

29   CHRIS: Seems like it to me. But maybe they only wanted to

30   borrow the salt.

31   JOHN: And the pepper.

32   ROBBIE: No way! Look, they have their own! *(They look.)*

33   CHRIS: You're right! Then it was us!

34   JOHN: Yeah, it was us!

35   ROBBIE: Which one of them do you think liked me?

1   CHRIS: The one who asked for the ketchup.

2   ROBBIE: But no one asked for the ketchup.

3   JOHN: Sorry, Robbie, it's just not your day.

4   ROBBIE: No, I think they both liked me! They were just too shy
5   to talk to me.

6   CHRIS: Well, why don't we find out?

7   ROBBIE: How?

8   CHRIS: Why don't we ask them if they'd like to come over here
9   and sit with us? Then we'll see who sits by who.

10 JOHN: Yeah! But first we need to put an empty chair by each of
11   us. *(They each put a chair beside them.)*

12 CHRIS: Now, which one of us is going to go over there and
13   invite them over?

14 ROBBIE: I volunteer!

15 JOHN and CHRIS: OK.

16 ROBBIE: *(Goes to the girls' table.)* Hi.

17 AMBER: Hi.

18 MEGAN: Hi.

19 ASHLEY: What? Would you like to borrow the ketchup?

20 ROBBIE: Uh ... yes! I want to borrow the ketchup!

21 MEAGAN: Here, we have two extra bottles, so take both.

22 ROBBIE: *(Takes the ketchup. Pause as he stares at them with a*
23   *bottle of ketchup in each hand.)* **Wow! Thanks!** *(Finally, he*
24   *leaves.)*

25 JOHN: So, what happened?

26 ROBBIE: *(Proudly holding up both bottles of ketchup.)* **Sorry**
27   **guys, but they both want me!**

28 CHRIS: Why, because they gave you two bottles of ketchup?

29 JOHN: Robbie, you need a reality check.

30 ROBBIE: No, no! You should've seen the way they were looking
31   at me! *(Imitates the girls.)* "Would you like to borrow the
32   ketchup? Here, take both." I'm telling you, they both want
33   me! But which one do I pick? *(The girls laugh out loud.)*

34 CHRIS: No, Robbie, they're laughing at you!

35 ROBBIE: They're not laughing at me!

1   **JOHN:** Man, just sit down and be cool.

2   **ROBBIE:** You don't understand. You didn't see the way they

3   looked at me. It's me they want! Me! *(MEAGAN and AMBER*

4   *go to the boys' table. They look at ROBBIE.)*

5   **AMBER:** Hi.

6   **MEAGAN:** Hi.

7   **ROBBIE:** Hi.

8   **AMBER:** Can we have the ketchup?

9   **ROBBIE:** *(Jumps up with a bottle of ketchup in each hand.)* **Oh,**

10   **baby! Can you have the ketchup? You bet you can have the**

11   **ketchup!** *(Holds out his arms. MEAGAN and AMBER give*

12   *him a strange look, each taking a bottle of ketchup.)*

13   **JOHN:** You girls want to sit with us?

14   **AMBER:** Sure, thanks. But we need to go get our stuff.

15   **MEAGAN:** We'll be right back.

16   **JOHN:** OK. *(ROBBIE rushes to get another chair to put by his. He*

17   *sits down with an empty chair on each side of him, anxiously*

18   *waiting for the girls to sit next to him. When the girls return,*

19   *MEAGAN sits by JOHN and AMBER sits by CHRIS. Seeing*

20   *this, ROBBIE stands up, looks at them, and then stomps off.*

21   *They all laugh.)*

The Babysitter

Cast (2 Male, 3 Female): Katie (9 years old),
Ricky (10 years old), April, Matt, Mom
Prop: Sidewalk chalk.
Setting: RICKY and KATIE's house.

1   *(AT RISE: RICKY is pulling his sister KATIE's hair.)*
2   **KATIE:** Stop it!
3   **RICKY:** Stop what?
4   **KATIE:** Stop pulling my hair! Stop it! *(Hits him.)*
5   **RICKY:** Ouch! Don't hit me! *(Hits her.)*
6   **KATIE:** Stop it! Don't hit me! *(Hits him.)*
7   **RICKY:** Then don't hit me! *(Hits her.)*
8   **APRIL:** *(Entering)* What's going on?
9   **KATIE:** Ricky hit me!
10   **RICKY:** She hit me first!
11   **APRIL:** OK, OK, that's enough. You two need to find something
12   to do. Katie, why don't you go in the backyard and play on
13   the swing set? And Ricky, why don't you go play with your
14   trucks?
15   **KATIE:** I don't want to go outside!
16   **RICKY:** I don't want to play with my trucks!
17   **APRIL:** Then what do you want to do?
18   **RICKY:** I want to ride my bike to Tim's house!
19   **KATIE:** And I want to make mud pies!
20   **APRIL:** Ricky, it's my responsibility to watch you, so you have
21   to stay here with me. And Katie, I don't think your mom
22   would be very pleased if she came home and found you
23   covered in mud.
24   **KATIE:** I hate having a babysitter! They never let us do
25   anything fun!
26   **APRIL:** That's not true.

117

1   RICKY: Yes it is!

2   APRIL: Now, you two be sweet and play with your toys.

3   KATIE: But I want to make mud pies!

4   RICKY: And I want to ride my bike to Tim's!

5   APRIL: Well, I'm sorry. No mud pies and no going over to

6   Tim's.

7   KATIE: Then can I make cupcakes? I know how!

8   RICKY: And can I spray paint my bike green? I'll be really

9   careful!

10   APRIL: No cupcakes and no spray painting.

11   KATIE: *(Stomps her foot.)* You won't let us do anything fun!

12   APRIL: Look, why don't you go to your rooms and play quietly?

13   And don't make any messes, OK? We don't want your mom

14   getting mad at me, do we?

15   RICKY: She'll be mad if we tell her how you mean you were!

16   KATIE: I want to make cupcakes! I want to make cupcakes! I

17   want to make cupcakes!

18   RICKY: And I want to spray paint my bike green!

19   APRIL: How about watching some TV?

20   KATIE: No! Cupcakes!

21   RICKY: No!

22   APRIL: A game of checkers?

23   KATIE: I hate checkers! *(Doorbell rings.)*

24   RICKY: Someone's here!

25   KATIE: I'll get it! *(Running Off)* I hope it's Mommy!

26   RICKY: *(Running after KATIE)* Mommy doesn't ring the

27   doorbell! *(A moment later, KATIE and RICKY enter the room*

28   *with MATT.)*

29   KATIE: *(Yelling)* April! Your boyfriend's here!

30   MATT: *(To APRIL)* Hey, I got your message: "Help!" So, here I

31   am.

32   APRIL: *(Pulls MATT away from the kids.)* Oh, they're driving me

33   crazy! They're the biggest brats I've ever seen! And if I

34   didn't need the money for band camp, I'd never baby-sit

35   those kids again!

1   MATT: Look, I'm great with kids, so just relax.

2   APRIL: Thanks, Matt.

3   MATT: So guys, what would you like to do?

4   KATIE: I want to make mud pies!

5   RICKY: And I want to ride my bike to Tim's. Or at least spray

6   paint it green!

7   MATT: Well, look what I brought over! Sidewalk chalk! *(Hands*

8   *it to them.)* How about if you both go outside and see who

9   can make the best picture? We'll have a contest!

10 KATIE: OK! *(Runs out.)*

11 RICKY: OK! *(Runs out.)*

12 APRIL: Wow. I'm impressed!

13 MATT: Glad I could help.

14 APRIL: You are wonderful! *(Gives him a hug.)* Thank you! Oh,

15   thank you so much!

16 MATT: You're welcome. So, when does Mrs. Patterson get

17   home?

18 APRIL: *(Looks at her watch.)* About two more hours.

19 MATT: Well, just think about the money.

20 APRIL: That's the only thing that's getting me through this!

21 MATT: And think about all the fun you'll be having at band

22   camp this summer.

23 APRIL: I wish you were going.

24 MATT: Well, if I knew how to play an instrument, I would.

25   *(They laugh.)* But I'll write you every day.

26 APRIL: And I'll do the same. *(RICKY and KATIE enter. KATIE is*

27   *crying. She has sidewalk chalk on her face and arms.)*

28 KATIE: Look what Ricky did to me!

29 RICKY: Yeah! I drew my picture on her!

30 KATIE: *(Hits RICKY.)* I hate you!

31 RICKY: *(Hits KATIE.)* Don't hit me!

32 APRIL: Come on, Katie, let's go get a wet rag.

33 MATT: I'll stay here with Ricky.

34 KATIE: I hate him!

35 APRIL: Come on, let's go. *(They exit.)*

1   RICKY: Matt, do you hate girls?

2   MATT: No, I like them.

3   RICKY: Well, I think girls are ugly and stupid! They never want

4   to do anything fun like play with cars or have bike races or

5   cut insects in half. All they want to do is play house or play

6   with stupid dolls!

7   MATT: Well, that's because God made boys and girls different.

8   RICKY: Well, I'm glad he didn't make me a girl! I hate girls!

9   Matt ... have you ever kissed a girl?

10 MATT: Uh ... well ... yeah.

11 RICKY: Ewwww! Yuckie! I bet you wanted to throw up!

12 MATT: Well, not really.

13 RICKY: Matt ... have you ever kissed our babysitter?

14 MATT: Uh ... yeah.

15 RICKY: Ewwww! Yuckie! How many times have you kissed her?

16 MATT: Oh, I don't know.

17 RICKY: A hundred times?

18 MATT: Maybe. I don't know.

19 RICKY: A thousand?

20 MATT: I don't know. I didn't count.

21 RICKY: A million billion times?

22 MATT: I said I didn't count. So ... what do you want to do?

23   *(APRIL and KATIE enter.)*

24 RICKY: *(Pointing at APRIL)* I want to see you kiss the babysitter!

25 KATIE: Yeah! I want to see that, too!

26 MATT: And I say let's think of something else to do.

27 APRIL: Definitely!

28 KATIE: *(Singing)* Matt and April sitting in a tree. K-I-S-S-I-N-G!

29   First comes love, then comes marriage, next comes April

30   with a baby carriage!

31 APRIL: Katie, that's enough!

32 RICKY: Tim told me that you could practice kissing by kissing

33   your arm like this. *(Kisses his arm.)* Is that what you do,

34   Matt?

35 APRIL: *(Laughing)* Yeah, is that what you do, Matt?

1 MATT: No!

2 KATIE: Come on, Matt! Kiss her!

3 RICKY: Yeah! We wanna see you kiss her!

4 MATT: Well, if I do, will you two promise to go outside and play

5   quietly? And no fighting?

6 RICKY and KATIE: We promise! We promise!

7 KATIE: Cross our hearts!

8 MATT: Well, what do you think, April? One little kiss?

9 APRIL: If it'll get them to play quietly, I say yes!

10 MATT: OK, you both really, really promise to be good from

11   now on if I kiss the babysitter?

12 RICKY and KATIE: Promise! We promise! *(MATT gives APRIL a*

13   *kiss as RICKY and KATIE watch, their eyes wide open. MOM*

14   *enters.)*

15 MOM: I'm home! I finished shopping early and I ... *(MATT and*

16   *APRIL jump apart.)*

17 APRIL: Oh, Mrs. Patterson, we were just ...

18 MOM: I saw what you were *just* doing in front of my sweet and

19   innocent children!

20 APRIL: But ...

21 MOM: And I can't believe what I'm seeing!

22 RICKY and KATIE: *(Rushing to MOM)* Mommy, you're home!

23 MATT: Really, Mrs. Patterson, you don't understand. See, it

24   was a dare from the kids. See, if I kissed April, then they

25   were going to go outside and play without fighting.

26 MOM: A dare, huh? Look, I know they would never think of

27   such a thing! Would you, sweethearts? *(They shake their*

28   *heads.)* Oh, my darlings, I don't know what you've been

29   exposed to, but you just forget about everything you've

30   seen, OK?

31 RICKY: Mommy, it was gross!

32 MOM: I know, sweetheart.

33 KATIE: I was scared!

34 APRIL: But Mrs. Patterson ...

35 MOM: April, you and your boyfriend may leave now! And

1   **believe me, I won't be calling you again. In fact, I may be**

2   **calling your parents!**

3 **APRIL: But ...**

4 **MOM: Good-bye!**

5 **MATT: But Mrs. Patterson ...**

6 **MOM: I *said* good-bye!** *(As MATT and APRIL exit, KATIE sticks*

7   *out her tongue at APRIL. APRIL sticks out her tongue at*

8   *KATIE.)*

9 **KATIE: Mommy, the babysitter stuck out her tongue at me.**

10 **MOM: Oh, I can't believe what a horrible babysitter she was to**

11   **my precious angels!**

12 **KATIE: Mommy, can we make cupcakes?**

13 **MOM: Of course we can, sweetheart.**

14 **KATIE: And can I go outside and decorate my bike?**

15 **MOM: *(Laughing)* Of course you can go outside and decorate**

16   **your bike, sweetheart.**

17 **KATIE: I love you, Mommy.**

18 **RICKY: I love you, too.**

19 **MOM: *(They all hug.)* Oh, and I love you, too!**

20 **KATIE: Cupcakes! Come on, Mommy!** *(MOM and KATIE exit.)*

21 **RICKY: And I'm going outside to decorate my bike!** *(As he*

22   *stands alone, he pantomimes spray painting in a wild*

23   *fashion.)*

Plays for
Six Actors

The Note

Cast (2 Male, 4 Female): Mrs. Brown, Tony, Mario,
Regina, Crystal, Debbie
Props: Chalk, paper and pens.
Setting: A classroom with five desks — three desks are in
the front row and two are in the back row.

1   *(AT RISE: CRYSTAL, REGINA, and DEBBIE sit in the front*
2   *desks, and TONY and MARIO sit in the back desks. MRS.*
3   *BROWN, the teacher, has her back to the students as she*
4   *is writing on the board. CRYSTAL passes a note to*
5   *REGINA, then REGINA passes a note back to CRYSTAL.*
6   *CRYSTAL passes a note to DEBBIE, and then DEBBIE*
7   *passes a note to REGINA. As CRYSTAL is passing a note to*
8   *REGINA, TONY grabs the note, reads it, and shows it to*
9   *MARIO. TONY and MARIO laugh quietly. REGINA passes*
10   *a note to CRYSTAL, then CRYSTAL passes a note to*
11   *DEBBIE, then DEBBIE passes a note back to CRYSTAL.)*
12 **MRS. BROWN:** *(Turning to the students)* **Now, does everyone**
13   **understand the assignment?**
14 **TONY:** *(Raising his hand)* **How long does it have to be?**
15 **MRS. BROWN: As long as it needs to be, Tony.**
16 **MARIO: Well, I can get my point across in one page.**
17 **MRS. BROWN: However, anything under twelve hundred**
18   **words will automatically result in a zero.**
19 **TONY: Twelve hundred words?**
20 **MARIO: That's a lot of words, Mrs. Brown!**
21 **MRS. BROWN: Students, this is Senior English. Please stop**
22   **acting so juvenile! Now, I'll give you the remainder of**
23   **the class period to work on your essays.** *(Exits.)*
24 **CRYSTAL: Tony, give me my note back!**
25 **TONY: What note?**

1 REGINA: Give it back, Tony!

2 MARIO: Tony doesn't have it. *(Holds up the note.)* I do!

3 DEBBIE: Give it back, Mario!

4 MARIO: *(Reading)* "And I think Matt is so hot! Any idea on
5   how I can get his attention?"

6 CRYSTAL: Shut up, Mario!

7 DEBBIE: Give her the note back!

8 REGINA: Yeah, give it back!

9 TONY: I know!

10 CRYSTAL: You know what?

11 TONY: How you can get Matt's attention.

12 REGINA: Stay out of it, Tony.

13 DEBBIE: Yeah, stay out of it!

14 MARIO: Tell me, Tony, how can she get Matt's attention?

15 TONY: Well, it's a bit complicated. Hey Crystal, you want to
16   take notes?

17 CRYSTAL: Shut up, Tony!

18 MARIO: Tell us, Tony! Tell us! We want to know how to get
19   Matt's attention!

20 TONY: OK, the way you get Matt's attention is ... Drum roll
21   please! *(MARIO makes a drum sound.)* Tell him that you
22   like him! Duh!

23 REGINA: Are you crazy?

24 DEBBIE: That'd be way too embarrassing!

25 REGINA: Yeah and what if he doesn't like her?

26 DEBBIE: Don't you understand how humiliating that
27   would be?

28 REGINA: And how could she ever look at him again?

29 DEBBIE: Or walk through the halls knowing that the guy
30   she loves can't stand her.

31 REGINA: A person can only take so much.

32 DEBBIE: So it's better to not know one way or the other.

33 REGINA: That's right. Like no news is good news.

34 DEBBIE: But what if he does like her, and you never get the
35   good news?

1   REGINA: But what if he doesn't?

2   DEBBIE: Should you take your chances?

3   REGINA: I don't know.

4   CRYSTAL: Can we all just forget about that stupid note? Please!

5   MARIO: Tony is right. You have to let him know you're
6   interested.

7   TONY: And if you're too shy to tell him yourself, then just leave
8   it up to us!

9   MARIO: That's right!

10   REGINA: No!

11   DEBBIE: No!

12   CRYSTAL: *(Jumps up.)* **No!**

13   TONY: Because we can show him this note, and it will save you
14   from going to all that trouble to figure out how to get his
15   attention. Believe me, this note will get his attention.

16   CRYSTAL: *(Tries to grab the note.)* And I say we *don't* show him
17   the note! Give me that! Give me that note!

18   TONY: I wish I could give it back, but ...

19   REGINA: Give her the note back, Tony!

20   DEBBIE: Yeah, give it back!

21   MARIO: Look girls, we're willing to do a little negotiating.

22   REGINA: You mean bribing?

23   MARIO: Well, we do need some help with our essays.

24   CRYSTAL: No way! I'm not writing either one of your essays!

25   TONY: *(Putting the note into his back pocket)* And who knows,
26   maybe things will turn out perfectly. Crystal likes Matt and
27   Matt likes Crystal. Except ...

28   CRYSTAL: What?

29   TONY: Did you know he has a girlfriend?

30   MARIO: Gosh, I hope she's not the jealous type.

31   CRYSTAL: You know what, go ahead and show him that note. I
32   don't care!

33   REGINA: Crystal, are you sure?

34   DEBBIE: He will. You know he will!

35   TONY: I'm that kind of guy. What can I say?

1   REGINA: Yeah, mean and cruel!
2   DEBBIE: What a jerk!
3   TONY: Hey, I like to have fun.
4   MRS. BROWN: *(Enters.)* **And how are we doing on our essays?**
5   *(They all begin writing. TONY passes a note to CRYSTAL, and*
6   *then CRYSTAL writes furiously and passes a note back to*
7   *TONY. TONY shows MARIO the note. REGINA and DEBBIE*
8   *each write notes and pass them to CRYSTAL.)*
9   MRS. BROWN: **Did I just see a note being passed?** *(Silence)* **How**
10   **many times have I said that passing notes is not, I repeat,**
11   ***not* acceptable in my class?**
12   CRYSTAL: It was me, Mrs. Brown. I'm sorry.
13   MRS. BROWN: **Well, Crystal, I appreciate your honesty. That**
14   **means a lot to me. Just let me have the note and we'll forget**
15   **it happened.**
16   CRYSTAL: Well, I don't have it. Tony grabbed it from my hand
17   and stuck it in his back pocket.
18   MRS. BROWN: **Tony, the note please!**
19   TONY: *(Stands, takes a piece of paper from his pocket, and hands*
20   *it to MRS. BROWN.)* **Sorry.**
21   MRS. BROWN: *(Looks at it.)* **Tony, this is your progress report**
22   **for your parents. The note, please!**
23   TONY: *(Reluctantly he gives her the note.)* **Here.**
24   MRS. BROWN: **Thank you. Now, sit down and work on your**
25   **essay.** *(Opens the note and reads it to herself.)* **Not to divulge**
26   **what's in this note, but Crystal, may I offer some advice?**
27   CRYSTAL: Uh ... yes ma'am.
28   MRS. BROWN: **Just tell him that you like him. Honesty is always**
29   **the best policy. Now, everyone get back to your essays. And**
30   **no more passing notes!** *(After a moment, the note passing*
31   *begins again. Each time MRS. BROWN turns in their*
32   *direction, they quickly freeze and pretend to be working on*
33   *the assignment. Finally, when MRS. BROWN exits the room,*
34   *they begin fighting and arguing again over another*
35   *intercepted note.)*

Baby Talk

Cast (3 Male, 3 Female): Dwight, Chad, Steve,
Mom, Audra, Julie

Setting: School hallway.

1　*(AT RISE: DWIGHT and STEVE approach CHAD, who talks*
2　　*like a baby.)*
3　**DWIGHT:** *(Approaching CHAD)* **Hey, you're a new student,**
4　　**aren't you?**
5　**CHAD: Uh-huh. I'm Chad.**
6　**DWIGHT: Man, are you trying to make Mr. Fritz mad, or what?**
7　**STEVE: Maybe you're trying to be the class clown and get some**
8　　**laughs, but believe me; Mr. Fritz is not the teacher to mess**
9　　**with.**
10　**DWIGHT: Yeah, it was funny at first, but after awhile, it got a**
11　　**little irritating.**
12　**CHAD: I don't know what I did.**
13　**STEVE: You don't know what you did? Man, you're talking like**
14　　**a baby!**
15　**DWIGHT: Don't get mad for me asking, but are you a little, you**
16　　**know – mentally challenged?**
17　**CHAD: Mentally challenged?**
18　**STEVE: It's OK. We understand. Have a nice life.** *(To DWIGHT)*
19　　**Come on; let's get out of here. They'll probably have him**
20　　**moved into another class by tomorrow.**
21　**CHAD: Wait! I'm not a dummy!**
22　**DWIGHT: Well, you talk like a dummy!**
23　**STEVE: Like a baby!**
24　**CHAD: But I've always talked this way.**
25　**STEVE: So where did you go to school last year?**
26　**CHAD: I didn't. At least not to public school.**
27　**DWIGHT and STEVE: What? Why?**
28　**CHAD: Well, my mom was overprotective and she home**

129

1   schooled me.

2   DWIGHT: So that's why you talk like a baby?

3   STEVE: I bet his mom talked to him like a baby for so long that

4   he doesn't know any better.

5   CHAD: But I didn't know I talked like a baby.

6   DWIGHT: Man, just listen to yourself!

7   CHAD: OK. So, do I sound like a baby?

8   DWIGHT and STEVE: *Yes!*

9   CHAD: Wow. This isn't cool, is it?

10   STEVE: No, it's not cool! Especially if you don't want to get beat

11   up!

12   DWIGHT: Or if you plan on getting a girlfriend! Think about it.

13   Do you think a girl's going to go out with a guy who talks

14   like a baby?

15   CHAD: I don't know.

16   DWIGHT: Trust us, she won't!

17   STEVE: But we're going to help you get past this.

18   DWIGHT: We are?

19   STEVE: Yeah! We'll be your coaches! Remember the movie *My*

20   *Fair Lady*?

21   DWIGHT: No.

22   CHAD: No.

23   STEVE: Well, this is going to be "My Fair Baby"!

24   DWIGHT: What?

25   STEVE: You know! Remember how Henry Higgins taught Eliza

26   Doolittle how to speak properly?

27   DWIGHT: Man, I missed that one.

28   STEVE: Well, just follow my lead.

29   DWIGHT: OK.

30   STEVE: So, can you stay here for a while?

31   CHAD: Well, my mom's right over there waiting to pick me up.

32   DWIGHT: Well, ask her if you can stay here and hang out with

33   us, OK?

34   CHAD: OK. Wait, here she comes.

35   MOM: *(Enters, talking like a baby to CHAD.)* Oh, there you are!

1   Did you have a good day at school today, sweetie?

2 CHAD: Uh-huh.

3 MOM: And did you miss your mommy?

4 CHAD: Uh ... I guess.

5 DWIGHT and STEVE: Mommy?

6 MOM: OK, sweetheart, let's go home now. Mommy will fix you

7   a healthy snack. How about some raisins on a log?

8 DWIGHT and STEVE: Raisins on a log?

9 MOM: Oh boys, you know! Celery sticks covered with peanut

10   butter with raisins on top. My sweet Chad here loves to

11   make them himself. *(Laughs.)* The raisins look like little

12   ants on a log!

13 CHAD: Uh, Mom ... can I stay here with my friends?

14 MOM: You want to stay after school and play with your little

15   friends?

16 CHAD: Uh-huh.

17 MOM: Well, I guess that would be all right. I'll come back here

18   in about an hour to pick you up.

19 CHAD: OK.

20 MOM: But remember ...

21 MOM and CHAD: Don't talk to strangers!

22 MOM: *(Pinches his cheek.)* Oh, you're such a good boy! *(Exits.)*

23 DWIGHT: Chad, does your mom always treat you like that?

24 CHAD: Uh-huh.

25 STEVE: No wonder! I believe we've identified the problem.

26 CHAD: But I don't understand what's so bad.

27 DWIGHT: Look Chad, your mom's always kept you at home

28   and treated you like a baby.

29 STEVE: You haven't been exposed to the real world! And

30   because of the way your mom talks to you, you only know

31   how to talk like a baby!

32 CHAD: So I really sound like a baby?

33 DWIGHT and STEVE: Yes!

34 CHAD: Then you guys have got to help me. And fast!

35 STEVE: OK, OK, we will.

1   **DWIGHT:** Yeah, just sit down and relax. *(To STEVE)* Now what
2   do we do? *(AUDRA and JULIE enter.)*
3   **AUDRA:** *(To CHAD)* Hi! Are you that new student? I'm Audra,
4   and this is my friend Julie. We're both cheerleaders here
5   at school. So, what's going on?
6   **STEVE:** Just talking!
7   **DWIGHT:** Yeah and we've got some important things to
8   discuss here so maybe we'll catch up with you girls later,
9   OK?
10   **JULIE:** Why are you trying to get rid of us?
11   **AUDRA:** Yeah, what's the big secret?
12   **CHAD:** There's no big secret. My friends here are just trying to
13   help me.
14   **AUDRA:** With homework?
15   **CHAD:** No, not homework. Something else. Something very
16   important.
17   **JULIE:** Why are you talking like a baby?
18   **CHAD:** I guess everyone notices.
19   **JULIE:** Are you one of those slow kids?
20   **STEVE:** No, he's not. The problem is that his mom home
21   schooled him and he's never been around *normal* people.
22   **AUDRA:** Huh?
23   **STEVE:** His mom always talked to him like he was a baby and
24   that's all he knows how to do.
25   **JULIE:** Oh.
26   **AUDRA:** Then it's not his fault. He can't help it.
27   **DWIGHT:** And we were about to help him learn how to talk
28   normal so he won't make a fool out of himself.
29   **CHAD:** Or get beat up.
30   **JULIE:** Oh! Can we help?
31   **AUDRA:** Yeah, let us help! *(The girls sit down by CHAD, one on*
32   *each side. He likes this.)*
33   **JULIE:** Don't be embarrassed, Chad.
34   **AUDRA:** Yeah, we're here to help you.
35   **STEVE:** OK, Chad, repeat after me. *(In a deep, masculine voice)*

1   Hey, what's up?

2 **CHAD:** *(Trying, but still sounding like a baby)* **Hey, what's up?**

3 **STEVE:** **OK, OK, try this. The rain in Spain stays mainly on the**
4   **plains.**

5 **DWIGHT:** **Steve, are you trying to confuse him?**

6 **STEVE:** **Just trust me.**

7 **CHAD:** **The rain in Spain stays ... uh ... stays where?**

8 **JULIE:** **Why don't you let us try?**

9 **STEVE:** **You think you can do any better?**

10 **JULIE:** **Of course we can.** *(Takes his hand, looks into his eyes,*
11   *and talks to him sweetly.)* **Now, Chad, all you have to do is**
12   **talk the way big people do, OK?**

13 **DWIGHT:** **Big people! You're funny, Julie.**

14 **STEVE:** **That's not going to help.**

15 **AUDRA:** *(Takes his other hand.)* **Like someone big and strong**
16   **that you admire. Like Superman!**

17 **DWIGHT:** **Superman! Please!**

18 **STEVE:** **You're wasting your time.**

19 **JULIE:** *(To CHAD)* **You think you can do that?**

20 **CHAD:** *(Looks at both girls several times as they are encouraging*
21   *him. He stands up. A pause, then he talks in a deep and*
22   *normal voice.)* **Talk like Superman. How was that?**

23 **DWIGHT:** **That's great!**

24 **STEVE:** **I think he's got it! I think he's got it! And again!**

25 **CHAD:** *(Deep voice)* **Talk like Superman.**

26 **DWIGHT:** **He's got it!**

27 **STEVE:** **Now try to say something else.**

28 **DWIGHT:** **Like ... Hey man, what's up?** *(AUDRA and JULIE stand,*
29   *each holding onto CHAD's hands.)*

30 **AUDRA:** **You can do it, Chad.**

31 **JULIE:** **We know you can.**

32 **CHAD:** *(Looks back and forth at the girls, then speaks in a deep*
33   *voice.)* **Hey man, what's up?**

34 **STEVE:** **He's got it!**

35 **DWIGHT:** **Way to go, Chad!** *(The girls hug CHAD as he smiles.)*

1   **JULIE: That was terrific.**

2   **AUDRA: We knew you could do it!**

3   **CHAD:** *(Lifting his arms in the air)* **Superman, to save the day!**

Four Boyfriends

Cast (4 Male, 2 Female): Lisa, Brooke, Eric, James, Danny, Phillip

Prop: A small, wrapped gift.

Setting: A mall.

1 LISA: Brooke, I've heard of a two-timer before, but this is
2   going way too far!
3 BROOKE: Lisa, you don't understand! Eric, James, Danny,
4   and Phillip all think they're the only one.
5 LISA: But four boyfriends? Four?
6 BROOKE: What's the problem? They're happy, I'm happy.
7   And believe me, with four boyfriends, I'm really happy!
8 LISA: I'm warning you, Brooke, you're gonna get caught.
9 BROOKE: How? They all go to different schools. Besides,
10   I'm smarter than you think. I know exactly how to play
11   this game.
12 LISA: And you're gonna lose this game, Brooke. Just don't
13   say I didn't warn you.
14 BROOKE: Think about it. Do I ever have to stay at home on
15   a Friday or Saturday night? No! Do I ever lack a date?
16   No! I can take my pick of what I want to do and who I
17   want to do it with.
18 LISA: Then tell me something, Brooke. Why are you here at
19   the mall with me?
20 BROOKE: Lisa, you're my best friend!
21 LISA: Wait a minute. I just thought of something.
22 BROOKE: What?
23 LISA: Well, if you can have four boyfriends at once, then
24   maybe, just maybe ...
25 BROOKE: What?
26 LISA: Maybe I'm not your *only* best friend!

1   BROOKE: Lisa!

2   LISA: Maybe you keep all your best friends separated, too!

3   BROOKE: Oh, don't be ridiculous! You're my one and only

4   best friend! B-F-F! Best friends forever!

5   LISA: OK, but make sure you keep it that way. *(ERIC enters.)*

6   ERIC: Hey, Brooke!

7   BROOKE: Eric! What are you doing here? I mean ... I'm glad

8   to see you, it's just ... I'm surprised to see you.

9   ERIC: I'm surprised to see you, too, Brooke.

10   LISA: Oh, you must be one of her ... I mean ... her one and

11   only!

12   ERIC: *(Smiling proudly)* That's me!

13   BROOKE: Uh, Eric, I thought you had some sort of family

14   celebration tonight. Your sister's birthday?

15   ERIC: Brooke, I don't have a sister!

16   BROOKE: Oh! What was I thinking? I was, uh ... thinking of

17   someone else.

18   ERIC: Remember, I wanted to take you to a movie tonight?

19   BROOKE: Oh, of course! I remember!

20   LISA: Oh, this must be my fault. For weeks now I've been

21   pestering Brooke to spend some time with me.

22   ERIC: You mean you've been pestering Brooke to spend

23   *every* weekend with you!

24   LISA: What?

25   ERIC: Well, it seems like every time I want to do something

26   with Brooke, she can't because of you! In fact, I think

27   you spend more time with her than I do!

28   LISA: I do not! This is the first weekend in a long time that

29   we've ...

30   BROOKE: Lisa!

31   LISA: I mean, I mean ... what do I mean? I mean, I don't

32   mean to keep her from you. That's what I mean.

33   ERIC: Man, something here doesn't seem right. Brooke,

34   you're not cheating on me, are you?

35   BROOKE: Eric, I would never cheat on you! I love you!

1 ERIC: OK, OK. I'm sorry for asking.
2 BROOKE: Eric, would you like to hang out with us for a
3   while?
4 ERIC: Sure! Maybe we could head over to the arcade. I'll
5   challenge both of you girls to a game.
6 BROOKE: Great!
7 LISA: Yeah, that sounds like fun. *(ERIC takes BROOKE's*
8   *hand. Just as they are about to leave, JAMES enters.)*
9 JAMES: Hey, baby!
10 BROOKE: *(Quickly pulls her hand away.)* **James!**
11 LISA: Number two?
12 ERIC: Number two?
13 BROOKE: I can't believe this is happening to me! I'm going
14   to die right here!
15 LISA: And miss all this fun? Remember, I tried to warn you!
16 BROOKE: Well, now you can help me!
17 LISA: And isn't it just great to meet new friends? Brooke
18   has more friends than anyone I know! You can't walk
19   through the mall without running into one of her
20   friends!
21 JAMES: Yes, my sweetheart has a great personality! I can't
22   deny that!
23 ERIC: *Your* sweetheart?
24 BROOKE: I'm dead!
25 LISA: And isn't it just great how everyone thinks of Brooke
26   as their ... as their sweet little sister! Yeah! Sweetheart
27   little sister!
28 ERIC: I didn't know that.
29 JAMES: Me, neither. Uh, Brooke, can I talk to you for a
30   minute?
31 BROOKE: Sure. *(She follows JAMES to the side.)*
32 JAMES: Why were you holding that guy's hand?
33 BROOKE: Because ... his hands were cold!
34 JAMES: I thought I was your one and only!
35 BROOKE: James, I would never cheat on you! I love you!

1   JAMES: Promise?

2   BROOKE: I promise.

3   JAMES: All right. *(They go back to the others.)* **So, what are y'all**

4   **up to?**

5   ERIC: Well, we were about to head over to the arcade. You

6   want to come with us?

7   JAMES: Sure!

8   BROOKE: Great!

9   LISA: *(Nudging BROOKE)* **Isn't this fun?** *(DANNY enters.)*

10   DANNY: Hi, Brooke!

11   BROOKE: Danny! Oh, no! This can't be happening to me!

12   LISA: Number three?

13   BOYS: Number three?

14   BROOKE: If I could just disappear!

15   LISA: And miss all this fun? *(Extends her hand to DANNY.)* **Hi!**

16   **I'm Lisa, Brooke's one and only best friend in the whole**

17   **world!**

18   DANNY: *(Shakes her hand.)* **I've heard a lot about you. I'm**

19   sorry to hear about all of your problems.

20   LISA: My problems?

21   BROOKE: Danny, this isn't a good time! So, what are you up

22   to?

23   LISA: No, wait! I'd like to hear about *all of my problems*!

24   BROOKE: Look, I don't think this is a good time.

25   LISA: Well, I do! So, Danny ... what do you think I should do?

26   You know, about all of my problems!

27   DANNY: Well, first of all, I think you should quit threatening

28   to run away from home. It upsets Brooke to hear you talk

29   about it. And it seems as though every weekend Brooke is

30   tied down to you because you're having another crisis in

31   your life! You shouldn't treat your friends like that!

32   LISA: I absolutely agree!

33   ERIC: Brooke, you are a great friend.

34   JAMES: I agree. Seems like there's just not enough of you to go

35   around!

1 LISA: Oh, you're right about that!

2 BROOKE: So, are we going to the arcade, or what?

3 LISA: But I wonder if Brooke has too many friends? It's

4   hard if you spread yourself too thin. Don't you agree?

5 ERIC: I think you have to set priorities.

6 DANNY: That's right. You can't just drop everything every

7   time a friend has a crisis. Especially when it's just for

8   attention.

9 JAMES: I agree.

10 LISA: Need for attention. So that's my problem! Gosh,

11   Brooke, you are a great friend!

12 DANNY: Hey, Brooke, could I talk to you for a second?

13 BROOKE: Sure. *(She follows DANNY to the side.)*

14 DANNY: What's going on? Who are those other two guys?

15 BROOKE: Oh, they're just some guys I'm trying to hook up

16   with Lisa.

17 DANNY: Both of them?

18 BROOKE: Well, one of them! She gets to decide who she

19   likes the best.

20 DANNY: Brooke, you're not cheating on me, are you?

21 BROOKE: Danny, I would never cheat on you! I love you!

22 DANNY: OK. *(They return to the group. PHILLIP enters.)*

23 PHILLIP: Hey, Beautiful! I've got a present for you!

24 BOYS: *(Except Phillip)* A present?

25 BROOKE: *(Grabs the present and hides it behind her back.)*

26   It's no big deal!

27 PHILLIP: No big deal?

28 BROOKE: Let's do this later, OK?

29 LISA: Number four?

30 BOYS: Number four?

31 BROOKE: I can't believe this is happening to me!

32 PHILLIP: So, what's going on?

33 LISA: Oh, we were about to head over to the arcade. You

34   want to come with us?

35 PHILLIP: Sure.

1   **BROOKE:** Thanks, Lisa!

2   **LISA:** You bet, best friend!

3   **PHILLIP:** Oh, so you're Lisa?

4   **LISA:** Yes. Why?

5   **PHILLIP:** Are you doing better now? I mean, Brooke told

6   me all about it. We don't keep any secrets from each

7   other, you know.

8   **LISA:** Oh, no! Of course not!

9   **BROOKE:** Phillip, don't. This isn't a good time.

10   **PHILLIP:** I'm sorry. I didn't mean to bring it up.

11   **LISA:** No, not at all! This is the perfect time.

12   **PHILLIP:** Well, I know it's been hard.

13   **LISA:** Of course. It's been very hard.

14   **PHILLIP:** Is the medication working?

15   **LISA:** I'm not sure. I wish I knew.

16   **ERIC:** Brooke, is she sick or something? *(All the BOYS begin*

17   *to step away from LISA.)*

18   **JAMES:** What's wrong with her?

19   **DANNY:** Is it contagious?

20   **BROOKE:** Oh, I'm beginning to feel sick.

21   **PHILLIP:** It's not contagious!

22   **DANNY:** Thank goodness!

23   **ERIC:** What does she have?

24   **JAMES:** Yeah, what do you have?

25   **PHILLIP:** Look, I'm sorry I brought this up. I guess I

26   thought they all knew. It's just whenever Brooke and I

27   try to plan something; she's always rushing to the

28   hospital to help you out.

29   **LISA:** Well, what can I say? She's a great friend!

30   **PHILLIP:** Is that a wig you're wearing? She told me your

31   hair was falling out.

32   **DANNY:** No wonder you want to run away from home!

33   **JAMES:** That's a wig?

34   **ERIC:** It looks real.

35   **LISA:** Well, what can I say?

1 BROOKE: Hey are we going to the arcade, or what?

2 PHILLIP: Yeah, let's go!

3 LISA: Sounds good to me! Maybe those games will help rid
4 my mind of all my problems! But I just hope my wig
5 doesn't fall off! Sometimes I get really excited when I
6 play those games.

7 PHILLIP: It's OK, Lisa. We understand.

8 ERIC: Yeah, we wouldn't laugh at you or anything.

9 DANNY: Yeah. We could even help you hold onto your wig if
10 you wanted us to.

11 LISA: Thanks! Gosh, all this attention! This is great!

12 BROOKE: So, are we going, or what?

13 PHILLIP: Let's go!

14 LISA: But wait! Are all of you guys taken? I mean, do you all
15 have a girlfriend? I sure hope not!

16 ERIC: I'm taken.

17 JAMES: Me too.

18 DANNY: Same here.

19 PHILLIP: Steady as they come.

20 LISA: Oh, darn! It's just you are all so cute!

21 BROOKE: *Let's go!*

22 LISA: But wait! At least you guys can tell me your
23 girlfriend's name.

24 ERIC: Brooke.

25 JAMES: Brooke.

26 DANNY: Brooke.

27 PHILLIP: Brooke.

28 BOYS: Brooke?

29 BROOKE: *Lisa!*

30 LISA: Brooke! Wow! Can you believe that? Is that a
31 coincidence or what?

32 ERIC: I guess it's a common name.

33 JAMES: I guess.

34 DANNY: Seems strange, though.

35 PHILLIP: Yeah, very strange.

1 LISA: And to think all four of you are standing right here
2   with my very best friend in the whole world ... *Brooke*!
3   What a name!
4 ERIC: I'm beginning to wonder if this is more than just a
5   coincidence.
6 JAMES: Me, too!
7 LISA: And you guys are so smart, too! Aren't they smart,
8   Brooke?
9 PHILLIP: Are you really sick? You don't look sick.
10 DANNY: I think you were teasing us about that wig. *(Yanks*
11   *on her hair.)*
12 LISA: Ouch!
13 BROOKE: Are we going to the arcade, or what?
14 LISA: But wait, Brooke! I thought you were supposed to
15   meet your boyfriend over there by the water fountain.
16 PHILLIP: Wait a minute! I'm Brooke's boyfriend!
17 DANNY: You've got that wrong! I am!
18 JAMES: What's going on here? Brooke's my girlfriend!
19 ERIC: And I thought I was the only one!
20 LISA: But wait, guys! Don't get upset! Brooke's such a
21   lovable person! Surely there's enough of her to go
22   around!
23 PHILLIP: No, thanks.
24 DANNY: What a joke!
25 JAMES: I'll pass!
26 ERIC: Me, too!
27 PHILLIP: Come on, guys. Let's go to the arcade.
28 DANNY: Yeah, maybe we can all find a *new* girlfriend.
29 JAMES: Sounds good to me.
30 ERIC: Me, too.
31 BROOKE: Wait! Wait! Don't be mad! *(The BOYS frown at*
32   *her.)*
33 LISA: That's too bad, Brooke. But hey, maybe you can go to
34   the arcade and find some new boyfriends.
35 BROOKE: Funny, Lisa.

1   **LISA: And maybe I can go and find me a new best friend in**
2   **the whole world. See ya!**
3   **PHILLIP: Hey, Lisa! Want to come with us?**
4   **DANNY: Yeah, come with us!**
5   **LISA: Oh, this is so much fun!** *Four* **boys!** *(LISA and the*
6   *BOYS start Off.)*
7   **BROOKE: At least I got a present out of it.**
8   **PHILLIP: Hold up, guys.** *(Goes back to BROOKE and snatches*
9   *the present from her hand.)* **I want my present back!**
10   *(They exit.)*
11   **BROOKE: Lisa!**

There's Always Next Year

Cast (3 Male, 3 Female): Brittany, Debbie, Leo,
Gail, Alan, Clark
Setting: School gym.

1 BRITTANY: I can't believe I humiliated myself like that!
2 DEBBIE: Brittany, you looked great out there. I don't understand
3   why you didn't make it as cheerleader. Leo's the one who
4   humiliated himself!
5 BRITTANY: Why am I so surprised? It's not about talent, but about
6   popularity! I could've had the best cheer and the most spirit,
7   but when it's left up to the students to vote, well, you saw what
8   just happened.
9 DEBBIE: Brittany, there's always next year.
10 BRITTANY: Next year? I'm not going to humiliate myself like that
11   again next year! Besides, do you think I'll be any more popular
12   next year?
13 DEBBIE: Maybe.
14 BRITTANY: Maybe if I get a new personality.
15 LEO: *(Enters, chanting)* Way to go Tigers, way to go! Way to go
16   Tigers, way to go! Way to go tigers, way to go!
17 DEBBIE: Congratulations, Leo.
18 LEO: Hey Brittany, sorry you didn't make it. But you know, there's
19   always next year.
20 BRITTANY: I'm not trying out again next year, Leo!
21 LEO: Yeah, I understand. It's hard to put your heart into
22   something and then be told you're not good enough.
23 DEBBIE: Leo, why don't you just shut up?
24 LEO: What? What did I say? Brittany, did I hurt your feelings? Look,
25   I'm sorry. *(Moves to the side to stretch and practice his cheers.)*

1   GAIL: *(Enters.)* Brittany, I'm so sorry you didn't make it. You looked
2   really good out there.
3   BRITTANY: Obviously not as good as Leo.
4   GAIL: No, actually you looked better than Leo. Really! You should
5   think about trying out again next year.
6   BRITTANY: I'm not trying out again! I'm through!
7   GAIL: Well, if you do, you can count on my vote.
8   BRITTANY: Thanks, Gail.
9   ALAN: *(Enters and goes to LEO.)* Leo, I can't believe you tried out for
10   cheerleader! I mean, there's not too many guys who want to
11   be a cheerleader.
12   LEO: What can I say? I'm just naturally good at this stuff.
13   ALAN: Well, you're definitely fun to watch. Me and the other guys
14   were laughing our heads off!
15   LEO: Laughing your heads off?
16   ALAN: Yeah, watching you do all those cute little moves! *(Tries to*
17   *imitate.)*
18   LEO: Cute little moves? Those moves are difficult and complicated!
19   It's not as easy as it looks!
20   ALAN: Yeah, right. Hey, Brittany, sorry you didn't make it. You
21   should think about trying out again next year.
22   BRITTANY: I'm not trying out next year! *(They watch as LEO*
23   *practices some moves.)*
24   DEBBIE: Unbelievable.
25   GAIL: He's so bad.
26   BRITTANY: Then I must have been worse.
27   DEBBIE: No, Brittany, you were great!
28   GAIL: A hundred times better than Leo.
29   BRITTANY: Well, the student body sure didn't think so.
30   CLARK: *(Enters and goes to LEO and ALAN.)* Leo, Leo, my man!
31   You're gonna introduce me to some of those cheerleaders,
32   aren't you?
33   LEO: Sure!
34   CLARK: And what a friend you are! Hey, are you gonna have
35   your own little set of pompoms? *(Imitating)* Go Tigers, go!

1   Go Tigers, go!

2   LEO: No, of course not. I'm there to catch the girls when they

3   fall out of their pyramids.

4   CLARK: But you'll be doing some cheers, too, won't you?

5   LEO: Well, yeah. Of course.

6   ALAN: Hey, why don't you do one for us, Leo?

7   LEO: Right now?

8   ALAN: Yeah!

9   CLARK: Yeah! *(They all watch as LEO does a very bad cheer.*

10   *BRITTANY glares at him as the others try to keep from*

11   *laughing.)*

12 LEO: And what is so funny?

13 BRITTANY: Sorry to break it to you, Leo, but you're terrible!

14   Terrible! And would anyone here like to tell me how Leo

15   was voted as cheerleader and I wasn't?

16 ALAN: Because he's fun to watch!

17 CLARK: Yeah! The pep rallies will be a barrel of laughs!

18 GAIL: Unless of course he gets really good over the summer.

19 DEBBIE: You mean the students voted for Leo because he's

20   bad?

21 CLARK: Yes! He's hilarious!

22 LEO: That's not true!

23 ALAN: Sorry, but it's true.

24 BRITTANY: And they didn't vote for me and I was good? He

25   beat me because he was bad?

26 CLARK: Funny is the key word here!

27 LEO: It wasn't funny!

28 ALL: *(Except BRITTANY and LEO)* Yes it was!

29 LEO: This is not funny!

30 CLARK: Yeah it is! Picture Leo holding his pompoms while

31   jumping up and down yelling, "Go Tigers! Go Tigers!"

32 LEO: I don't get pompoms!

33 BRITTANY: Everyone gets pompoms, Leo!

34 ALAN: You know, this is the first year for our school to have a

35   boy cheerleader.

1 LEO: So? I like to start new trends!

2 ALAN: And we'll be there to support you all the way, Leo!

3 CLARK: Yeah, laughing our heads off at every pep rally! *(They*
4   *all laugh.)*

5 BRITTANY: Hey, leave him alone. At least he had the courage
6   to try out.

7 DEBBIE: And he probably will get better over the summer
8   months.

9 GAIL: A lot better.

10 LEO: Yeah, so leave me alone!

11 CLARK: Hey, I'm sorry.

12 ALAN: Yeah, me too.

13 CLARK: I'm sure you'll get really good this summer with all
14   those cheerleading camps.

15 ALAN: Yeah, you'll improve so much we won't have anything to
16   laugh about at the pep rallies.

17 LEO: You know, on second thought, I don't want to spend my
18   entire summer learning new cheers. Cheerleading
19   camps? I wasn't thinking about that.

20 GAIL: Well, Leo, that's what you'll be doing.

21 DEBBIE: That's right. All summer long.

22 ALAN: That's too bad, Leo.

23 CLARK: Yeah, we'll be down at the park on our skateboards.
24   Didn't you get a new skateboard?

25 LEO: Look, I've changed my mind, OK? I don't want to learn
26   new cheers all summer, and I don't want to be a
27   cheerleader. Yeah, I was the best, but no, I've changed my
28   mind!

29 ALAN: Smart move, Leo.

30 CLARK: Come on, Leo, let's go find Mrs. Morris and tell her
31   you've changed your mind.

32 LEO: Yeah, they'll just let the alternate step up and take my
33   place.

34 DEBBIE: Brittany, you were the alternate!

35 GAIL: That's right!

1   DEBBIE: Oh Brittany, this is great.

2   BRITTANY: Oh, my gosh!

3   LEO: Hey, you were pretty good, Brittany.

4   BRITTANY: Thanks, Leo.

5   CLARK: Congratulations, Brittany.

6   ALAN: Yeah, congratulations.

7   BRITTANY: Thank you! Oh, thank you, Leo.

8   ALAN: Hey, Leo, if you change your mind this summer and

9   wish you were learning new cheers instead of

10   skateboarding, you can always try out again next year.

11   LEO: Forget it, Alan. I know what my true talent is and that's

12   skateboarding! I'm the king of the ramp! *(The boys exit*

13   *and the girls jump up and down and scream.)*

Plays for More than Six Actors

Top Secret

Cast (6 Male, 5 Female): Greg, Jenny, Chris, Tina,
Sara, Mr. Moore, Tommy, Mrs. Biggs,
Mayor Parks, Fred, Sue

Props: Camera, pad of paper, pencil, hats, sunglasses.

1   *(AT RISE: GREG, JENNY and CHRIS enter.)*

2   **GREG:** I can't believe Mrs. Carter is making us write an essay

3   about our parents!

4   **JENNY:** I know. I mean, it'd be more fun to write about

5   someone famous rather than our boring parents.

6   **GREG:** *(As if writing)* "My parents ... there is nothing special

7   about them. Actually they are quite boring. My father is a

8   dentist and my mother ... well, she is just a mother. The

9   end."

10   **JENNY:** OK, my turn. "My parents ... if only they had a clue. To

11   them, fun is going out for ice cream. They've never done

12   anything spectacular ... except for having me. The end."

13   **CHRIS:** Way to go, guys. But remember, this essay has to be at

14   least twelve hundred words.

15   **GREG:** Twelve hundred words? Man!

16   **JENNY:** I can't think of a hundred words to write about my

17   parents! Oh wait, I know! My mother loves to gripe! It's

18   her favorite pastime. She gripes at me. She gripes at my

19   sister. She gripes at my father. She even gripes at the dog!

20   Maybe I could go on and on about that!

21   **GREG:** And my father is a couch potato! Every night and all

22   weekend long he's a zombie in front of the TV. I wonder if

23   I could list all the shows he likes to watch on TV? That'd

24   probably take up a couple hundred words.

25   **JENNY:** What about you, Chris? What are you going to write

26   about?

1 CHRIS: Me? Oh, that'll be easy.

2 JENNY: Why's that? Your parents special?

3 GREG: I doubt that! Chris' dad works at the Handy Hut.

4 CHRIS: That's true Greg, but you don't know the entire story
5   about my family.

6 JENNY: What story?

7 CHRIS: Well, my dad may seem like an ordinary man, but the
8   truth is, he's not. In fact, he's a very important person.

9 GREG: What? Manager of the Handy Hut?

10 CHRIS: Funny, Greg. As a matter of fact, my dad is partially
11   responsible for many of the decisions made in this
12   country.

13 GREG: Oh yeah, sure!

14 CHRIS: It's true.

15 GREG: Jenny, do you believe him?

16 JENNY: Of course not.

17 CHRIS: No, it's true. My dad is related to the President of the
18   United States.

19 GREG: Your dad who works at the Handy Hut?

20 CHRIS: That's right.

21 JENNY: Chris, are you teasing us?

22 CHRIS: No! It's true! I promise!

23 GREG: And just how is it that your dad is related to the
24   President? A forty-fifth cousin?

25 CHRIS: No. Look, never mind. I shouldn't even be telling you
26   this. It could get us into big trouble.

27 JENNY: Why?

28 CHRIS: Because it's top-secret information.

29 JENNY: Oh, come on, Chris. Tell us. Please!

30 GREG: Yeah, tell us. Please. I need a good laugh!

31 JENNY: Stop it, Greg! I think he's serious.

32 CHRIS: Well, maybe ... if you two swear, and I mean really
33   swear not to share this information with anyone. And I
34   mean *anyone*!

35 JENNY: I won't. I promise.

1   GREG: Hey, me too. My lips are sealed.

2   CHRIS: All right, then. My dad ... well, my dad is the President's

3   brother.

4   JENNY: Are you serious?

5   GREG: You're kidding, right?

6   CHRIS: No, it's true.

7   GREG: Oh, please! Your dad who works at the Handy Hut is the

8   President's brother?

9   CHRIS: Yes. And the only reason my dad works there is to keep

10   his identity a secret.

11   JENNY: Wow! That means the President of the United States is

12   your uncle?

13   CHRIS: That's right. He likes me to call him Uncle President.

14   GREG: Uncle President?

15   CHRIS: That's right.

16   JENNY: Wow! This is unbelievable!

17   GREG: That's right, Jenny. It is unbelievable.

18   JENNY: Just think, the President's brother lives right here in

19   our town!

20   GREG: Yeah, and he works at the Handy Hut! Wow. What do ya

21   know!

22   CHRIS: Like I said, it's a cover. We don't want people knowing

23   who we really are.

24   JENNY: Why not?

25   CHRIS: Because then the media would be all over us. They'd

26   never leave us alone.

27   JENNY: Well, I can understand that.

28   GREG: So Chris, have you ever been to the White House?

29   CHRIS: Oh sure. All the time. In fact, we'll be going again this

30   summer for our family reunion.

31   JENNY: Wow! I can't believe this!

32   GREG: Maybe you shouldn't believe this, Jenny.

33   CHRIS: Well, I've gotta run. I'd like to get home in time to talk

34   to Uncle President tonight. 'Bye.

35   JENNY: 'Bye.

1　GREG: 'Bye. *(They all exit. SARA and TINA enter. TINA has a*
2　　　*camera around her neck and carries a pad of paper and*
3　　　*pencil.)*
4　TINA: I've got to find Chris before anyone else does.
5　SARA: But we've looked everywhere.
6　TINA: And we have to keep looking. Tina, this is my chance!
7　　　The school paper has never had a story like this!
8　SARA: Tina, if you get this story, forget the school paper. Take
9　　　it straight to *The Herald*. I'm sure they'd pay you plenty
10　　　for a story like this.
11　TINA: You're right! My story on the front page of *The Herald*!
12　　　It'll be the beginning of my career as a journalist! *(CHRIS*
13　　　*enters.)*
14　SARA: Tina, look! There's Chris!
15　TINA: *(Rushes to him.)* Chris, hey, Chris! Can I take your picture
16　　　for the paper?
17　CHRIS: My picture? Why?
18　TINA: Smile! *(Snaps a picture.)*
19　CHRIS: Uh ... What's so special about me?
20　SARA: What's so special about you? Chris, you're just so cute!
21　CHRIS: I am?
22　TINA: Chris, can I ask you a few questions?
23　CHRIS: I guess.
24　TINA: Tell me about your family.
25　CHRIS: My family?
26　TINA: And don't leave *anything* out.
27　CHRIS: OK ... Uh ...
28　TINA: Did your dad and his brother fight much when they
29　　　were kids?
30　CHRIS: You want to know about my dad?
31　TINA: Yes, of course!
32　CHRIS: Well, let's see ... my dad and his brother ... yes, they
33　　　fought a lot.
34　TINA: And what sort of things did they fight about?
35　CHRIS: Well, my uncle was really bad about telling lies and it

1   always got my dad into trouble.

2   SARA: Really? Your uncle lied?

3   CHRIS: All the time. Heck, he still does.

4   TINA: *(Writing furiously)* **Is that right? What sort of things does**

5   **your uncle lie about?**

6   CHRIS: Oh, you name it! He even lies at work if it helps to

7   make him look good. Stretches the truth, exaggerates,

8   little white lies, you know!

9   TINA: *(Writing)* **Is that right?**

10   CHRIS: You bet. My uncle's real bad about making promises,

11   then turns around and does the opposite. He'll even laugh

12   about it later.

13   TINA: *(Writing)* **He laughs about his lies ...**

14   CHRIS: Yep. Heck, my uncle has even been known to steal

15   money. And the thing is, everybody at work knows about

16   it, but they just try to protect him from getting caught.

17   SARA: Probably because if he lost his job, they would, too.

18   CHRIS: Exactly!

19   TINA: This is going to be one powerful story!

20   CHRIS: If you ask me, they should put my uncle in prison.

21   TINA: *(Writing)* **Uh-huh ... should put him in prison.**

22   SARA: Tina, this story will make you a famous journalist. You'll

23   probably get calls for interviews after this.

24   CHRIS: Do you want to take some more pictures of me?

25   TINA: No thanks; I've got to get busy on this story. *(Kisses his*

26   *cheek.)* **Chris, thank you so much!**

27   CHRIS: Sure, but ...

28   SARA: *(Kisses his cheek.)* **You are just so cute!** *(TINA and SARA*

29   *exit.)*

30   CHRIS: But you didn't even ask any questions about me.

31   *(Smiles.)* **Well, I guess a picture is worth a thousand words.**

32   *(As he struts off)* **I'm so cute!** *(Exits. MR. MOORE, the school*

33   *principal and TOMMY, a student, enter.)*

34   MR. MOORE: Tommy, have you seen Chris?

35   TOMMY: No. Mr. Moore, is Chris in trouble?

1   **MR. MOORE:** Oh, no! No, no, no, no, no! Chris is a hero!

2   **TOMMY:** A hero?

3   **MR. MOORE:** Here I am the principal of this school and I will

4   soon be able to talk to the President himself! All because

5   of Chris! What a fine young man he is.

6   **TOMMY:** What president?

7   **MR. MOORE:** The President of the United States!

8   **TOMMY:** Chris knows him?

9   **MR. MOORE:** The President is Chris' uncle! And with that, I'll

10   be able to get a call into the President himself! In fact, I'm

11   planning to invite him to speak at the school on drug

12   prevention. How can the President refuse when his own

13   nephew attends this school?

14   **TOMMY:** Wow! I didn't know!

15   **MR. MOORE:** Yes, and afterwards the President and I can go

16   into my office and have a little chat. I'm sure he'd be

17   interested to hear my views on how to run this country. In

18   fact, I think I'll start him a list right now. *(MR. MOORE and*

19   *TOMMY exit. MAYOR PARKS and MRS. BIGGS enter.)*

20   **MRS. BIGGS:** Mayor Parks, I'm so excited. The awards ceremony

21   will be the talk of the town.

22   **MAYOR PARKS:** I will be honored to present Chris with the key

23   to our city.

24   **MRS. BIGGS:** I've called all the radio and TV stations. They all

25   plan to cover the ceremony.

26   **MAYOR PARKS:** Good, good. This will put our town on the

27   map. Perhaps we can look into a Presidential Museum in

28   the near future. Why, tourists will come from all over. Can

29   you imagine how this will boost our economy?

30   **MRS. BIGGS:** It's so exciting!

31   **MAYOR PARKS:** And as the Mayor of this town, I will contact

32   the President myself and invite him to attend the

33   ceremony.

34   **MRS. BIGGS:** Mayor Parks, do you think the President of the

35   United States will actually come here?

1   MAYOR PARKS: Yes, I do. I'm sure he'll be delighted to see his
2   nephew awarded with the key to our city.
3   MRS. BIGGS: This is just so exciting! Our town will never be
4   the same!
5   MAYOR PARKS: There's still so much to do before the
6   ceremony!
7   MRS. BIGGS: What can I do to help?
8   MAYOR PARKS: Help me find Chris so I can tell him the good
9   news. *(MAYOR PARKS and MRS. BIGGS exit. FRED and SUE,*
10   *CHRIS's parents, enter. They are wearing hats and*
11   *sunglasses.)*
12   FRED: I'm going to wring his neck!
13   SUE: How could Chris do this to us?
14   FRED: Our house has become a zoo! Reporters, cameras,
15   television crews!
16   SUE: You'd think we were celebrities!
17   FRED: All because of a stupid lie our son told!
18   SUE: Where could he be?
19   FRED: I don't know, but when I find him, oh, when I find
20   him ...
21   SUE: Come on! Let's get out of here! I see some more of those
22   reporters! *(They rush Off. CHRIS enters. After a moment,*
23   *SARA, TINA, MR. MOORE, TOMMY, MRS. BIGGS, and*
24   *MAYOR PARKS enter and rush to CHRIS.)*
25   TINA: Chris, Chris! Did you see my story in *The Herald* this
26   morning?
27   SARA: The editor has already offered Tina a job writing for
28   the paper! And she hasn't even graduated from high
29   school yet!
30   MRS. BIGGS: Chris, we finally found you!
31   TIMMY: So, Chris, how does it feel to be so popular?
32   MR. MOORE: Chris, I need your help. What's your uncle's
33   phone number? I need to call the President and invite him
34   to speak at our school.
35   MAYOR PARKS: Chris, next week we will have a ceremony and

1   present you with a key to the city.

2 CHRIS: Uh ... what's going on?

3 MRS. BIGGS: Sweetheart, we all know the truth. The President
4   is your uncle.

5 MAYOR PARKS: *(Patting his back)* Yes, and thanks to you, our
6   town will never be the same again. *(FRED and SUE enter
7   and rush to CHRIS.)*

8 FRED: Chris, what have you done this time?

9 SUE: You are in big trouble, young man!

10 MAYOR PARKS: *(To FRED)* Sir, it's a pleasure to meet you.

11 FRED: Keep your hands off of me! I've had enough of your
12   reporters!

13 MAYOR PARKS: Oh no! I'm not a reporter. I'm Mayor Parks.
14   And how is your brother doing?

15 SUE: Chris, when you get home, I want you to go straight to
16   your room!

17 CHRIS: But Mom ...

18 MR. MOORE: *(To FRED)* Sir, we're so proud of your son.

19 FRED: For lying? You're proud of my son for lying?

20 ALL: What?

21 FRED: All day long people have been banging on my door,
22   calling my home, calling my work ... all insisting that I'm
23   related to the President of the United States! Well, let me
24   tell you something! If I'm related to the President of the
25   United States, then you're all monkeys and don't know it!

26 ALL: What? It's not true?

27 CHRIS: *(Shrugs.)* It was just a little lie. *(ALL but CHRIS ad-lib "I
28   can't believe this," etc.)*

29 MAYOR PARKS: There goes the Presidential Museum.

30 TINA: So much for my career as a journalist! *(ALL but CHRIS
31   ad-lib as they exit "All this planning for nothing," etc.)*

32 CHRIS: Mom, Dad ... what can I say? *(He shrugs and smiles.)* I'm
33   sorry?

Dead or Alive

Cast (4 Male, 5 Female): Shelly, Erica, Rose, Craig, Nick, Kurt, Ted, Tiffany, Stormy

Prop: Hall pass.

Setting: The girls' bathroom.

1   *(AT RISE: SHELLY and ERICA run into the girls' bathroom.)*

2   SHELLY: Wow, I can't believe we did that!

3   ERICA: I've never done anything like this before.

4   SHELLY: Do you think the school will call our parents? *(As if*

5   *talking into a phone)* "Your child was present for first and

6   second period today, but has failed to show up for her

7   remaining classes. Please call the school as soon as

8   possible."

9   ERICA: They won't call. We'll just get an unexcused absence.

10 SHELLY: But when we show up tomorrow, won't they expect a

11 note from our parents or a doctor's excuse or something?

12 ERICA: Just say you forgot. Sor-ry! Look, Shelly, let's quit

13 worrying about tomorrow and just enjoy the moment,

14 OK?

15 SHELLY: You're right. So what do we do now?

16 ERICA: Go to the mall?

17 SHELLY: We can't do that. Someone will see us and know we're

18 supposed to be in school.

19 ERICA: Well, we can't hide out in this bathroom all day.

20 SHELLY: You want to go to the Burrito Shack and have a nice

21 long, leisurely lunch?

22 ERICA: Sure, but do you have any money? My mom sends a

23 check to the cafeteria so I don't have to keep up with the

24 money.

25 SHELLY: Oh, darn. I only have three dollars.

26 ERICA: OK, that idea is out.

1   ROSE: *(Enters carrying a pass.)* **What are y'all doing in here?**
2   **Skipping class?**
3   SHELLY: **Yep.**
4   ERICA: **You caught us in the act.**
5   ROSE: **Are you serious?**
6   SHELLY: **Yeah, but we can't figure out what to do now that**
7   **we've skipped third period. Any suggestions?**
8   ROSE: **Well for one, actually leave the school! You can't hide**
9   **out in the girls' bathroom all day! Go home and watch TV!**
10 ERICA: **Can't go to my house. My dad works nights and sleeps**
11   **days.**
12 SHELLY: **And I ride the bus, and my house is too far.**
13 ERICA: **So much for that idea.**
14 ROSE: **Walk to the movie theatre and catch a movie.**
15 ERICA: **We would if we had enough money.**
16 ROSE: **Wow, well y'all picked a bad day to skip. Nowhere to go,**
17   **nothing to do, no money ... plus ...**
18 SHELLY: **Plus what?**
19 ROSE: **Plus tomorrow when Mr. Hernandez figures out what**
20   **you two did, it's this ...** *(Using her finger, she imitates*
21   *cutting her throat.)* **Well, have fun. See ya.** *(Exits.)*
22 SHELLY: **Erica, I don't think this was such a great idea.**
23 ERICA: **I know. I'm beginning to think that, too. So what are**
24   **we supposed to do now? Sneak into third period?**
25 SHELLY: **Only with a good excuse as to why we're late.**
26 ERICA: **And we'll have to have the same excuse since we're**
27   **both in the same class.** *(CRAIG enters.)*
28 SHELLY: **Hey, what are *you* doing in here? This is the *girls'***
29   **bathroom!**
30 CRAIG: **I know, but Mrs. Jackson sent me out to look for you**
31   **two.**
32 ERICA: **She did?**
33 CRAIG: **Uh-huh. She said she checked the computer and saw**
34   **that you were both around for first and second period,**
35   **then disappeared for third. And since you two are best**

1 friends and have third period together, well, she figured
2 you were skipping. Smart lady, huh?
3 SHELLY: Erica, this was a really stupid idea! We finally get the
4   nerve up to skip school and what happens? We're caught
5   before we can even leave the school building. Not to
6   mention that we're practically trapped in the girls'
7   bathroom!
8 CRAIG: I can say I didn't find you.
9 ERICA: Yes! Say you never saw us!
10 CRAIG: Fine with me. I don't care. But what are you going to do?
11 NICK: *(Enters.)* **Oh, you found them!** *(Laughing as he points his*
12   *finger at them.)* **You two girls are in big trouble!**
13 CRAIG: Look Nick, we didn't find them, OK?
14 ERICA: That's right. You never saw us.
15 CRAIG: *(To Nick)* What did Mrs. Jackson do? Send you out to look
16   for them, too?
17 NICK: Heck, she sent the entire class out to look for them.
18 SHELLY: The entire class is looking for us?
19 NICK: Yep. And Mrs. Jackson said she had a gut feeling you girls
20   were hiding, and she wanted you found, dead or alive!
21 SHELLY: Dead or alive? Oh no, she must be really mad!
22 ERICA: And she dismissed the entire class to look for us?
23 NICK: Yep. Sorry.
24 CRAIG: Mrs. Jackson wants to prove a point. You know how she
25   is about that. Remember last week when three students
26   didn't turn in their DNA project?
27 ERICA: We're dead!
28 NICK: Yeah and she even offered a reward.
29 SHELLY: She offered a reward for our capture?
30 CRAIG: Hey, what is it? Maybe we do want to bring them in!
31 NICK: Whoever brings them back to class gets an extra hundred
32   points.
33 CRAIG: Boy, I could use an extra hundred. I kinda bombed on
34   that DNA project.
35 NICK: Me, too.

1   **ERICA:** Well, look, you never saw us, OK? *(KURT and TED begin*

2   *to enter.)*

3   **KURT:** Think they're in here?

4   **TED:** Hey Kurt, I'm not sure we should go into the girls'

5   bathroom.

6   **KURT:** We're on a mission. Come on! Well, what do you know?

7   We found them!

8   **TED:** All right! Let's cuff 'em and bring them in! Here comes

9   my extra hundred points! Yes!

10 **NICK:** Uh, we found them first.

11 **KURT:** You did?

12 **CRAIG:** You mean, I found them first!

13 **SHELLY:** Would it do any good to suggest that none of you ever

14   saw us?

15 **ERICA:** Please? *(The boys look at each other and consider this*

16   *idea.)*

17 **BOYS:** No.

18 **ERICA:** Gee, thanks.

19 **SHELLY:** Guess everyone is failing Mrs. Jackson's class.

20 **KURT:** Hey, maybe if we all bring them in, we'll all get an extra

21   hundred points.

22 **NICK:** Yeah. I bet Mrs. Jackson will go for that.

23 **TED:** Sounds good to me.

24 **CRAIG:** I guess we can try. *(TIFFANY and STORMY enter.)*

25 **TIFFANY:** Let's look in here. There they are!

26 **STORMY:** *(Looking at the boys)* What are you guys doing in

27   here? This is the *girls'* bathroom!

28 **KURT:** Look, we found them first.

29 **TED:** Yeah, and all four of us are taking them in.

30 **NICK:** Yeah, dead or alive!

31 **STORMY:** Well, they look alive to me.

32 **SHELLY:** Not for long.

33 **ERICA:** Shelly, don't say that!

34 **TIFFANY:** We need the extra credit, too. I got a fifty on that

35   stupid DNA project.

1 STORMY: So, can't we say that we *all* found them and *all* get
2   that extra hundred points?
3 KURT: No way.
4 TED: We were here first.
5 NICK: Actually, we were.
6 CRAIG: Actually, I was!
7 TIFFANY: But what's the big deal? We're *all* here now.
8 STORMY: And we *all* need that extra credit.
9 NICK: Well, maybe Mrs. Jackson doesn't want to give half the
10   class an extra hundred.
11 CRAIG: Then it should go to me because I was sent out first
12   and I found them first.
13 SHELLY: Look, forget all this. We're turning ourselves in.
14 ERICA: We are?
15 SHELLY: Yes. So none of you need to fight over who gets to drag
16   us back because we're going to do it ourselves.
17 ERICA: Are you sure about this?
18 SHELLY: I'm sure. So, all of you just go back to class and tell
19   Mrs. Jackson we're on our way. *(They all exit, mumbling*
20   *about not getting the extra credit.)*
21 ERICA: Now what?
22 SHELLY: Now we come up with the best excuse we can think
23   of. Something believable.
24 ERICA: I was throwing up and you were holding my hair?
25 SHELLY: She won't believe that.
26 ERICA: My mom died and you had to console me in the
27   bathroom? I can splash water on my face so my mascara
28   will run.
29 SHELLY: Erica, all she has to do is call your mom! Duh!
30 ERICA: Yeah, I didn't think about that. Uh ... I dropped my
31   contact on the bathroom floor and you were helping me
32   look for it?
33 SHELLY: That'd be good if you actually wore contacts!
34 ERICA: OK, then I had something in my eye and you were
35   helping me get it out!

1   SHELLY: And she'll say, "Erica, your eye's not even red!"

2   ERICA: OK, then what do we do?

3   SHELLY: I'm thinking.

4   ERICA: Well, hurry and think of something! Everyone will be

5   back to the class any minute now!

6   SHELLY: How about if we tell Mrs. Jackson the truth.

7   ERICA: The truth? How stupid is that?

8   SHELLY: Probably stupid enough to get us out of trouble. Mrs.

9   Jackson expects us to lie, right?

10 ERICA: Yeah.

11 SHELLY: But we'll surprise her and tell her the truth!

12 ERICA: And say we're really, really, really sorry and we learned

13   our lesson. *(SHELLY nods.)* That might actually work!

14 SHELLY: Well, come on, let's get this over with. You know, it

15   was still fun. I mean, now we can brag about how we

16   skipped class.

17 ERICA: Yeah! And how an entire class was even dismissed to

18   look for us! *Us!* Aren't we special!

19 SHELLY: *(As they exit)* Let's just leave out the part about how

20   we hid in the girls' bathroom the entire time.

21 ERICA: Good idea.

The Dance

Cast (4 Male, 4 Female): Meg, Jamie, Teresa, Darla,
Bryan, Chuck, Mike, Melvin
Props: Four pairs of handcuffs, nose spray, notepad,
pencil, trash can.
Setting: Outside of a school dance.

1   *(AT RISE: MEG, JAMIE, and TERESA are standing outside*
2   *the school building waiting to go inside for a dance.)*
3   **MEG: Anybody see her?**
4   **JAMIE: Not yet.**
5   **TERESA: Thank goodness!**
6   **JAMIE: Hey, maybe she came down sick! Wouldn't that be**
7   **great?**
8   **MEG: A miracle.**
9   **TERESA: A blessing.**
10 **DARLA:** *(Enters.)* **I'm here! Better late than never!**
11 **TERESA: We should've prayed.**
12 **DARLA: Oh, this dance is going to be great!**
13 **JAMIE: You're right. Maybe it's not too late.** *(Looks*
14   *heavenward.)* **Please, oh, please, let us keep our dates**
15   **tonight!**
16 **DARLA: So ... do we all have dates tonight?**
17 **MEG: We do. Do you, Darla?**
18 **DARLA: Me? Oh, you know that's not my style. It's more fun**
19   **to come alone and then decide who I want to dance**
20   **with.**
21 **TERESA: We know, Darla. Believe me, we know! Because**
22   **you always seem to go after one of our dates!**
23 **DARLA: Oh, don't be ridiculous.**
24 **MEG: Every time. It never fails.**
25 **DARLA: That's not true.**

1   MEG: Yes, it is!

2   JAMIE: Face it, Darla. You steal boyfriends.

3   DARLA: No, I don't!

4   TERESA: Can you believe it? She denies it.

5   JAMIE: I believe it.

6   DARLA: *(Looking around)* So ... where are your boyfriends?

7   MEG: We hid them!

8   DARLA: What?

9   JAMIE: That's right. We hid them. That way, Darla, we don't
10   have to worry about you trying to steal them.

11 DARLA: *(Laughing)* Oh, don't be so silly. I never steal
12   boyfriends. I just ... I just borrow them for a little while.

13 TERESA: Well, tonight that's not going to happen.

14 DARLA: Why not, Teresa? Are you so insecure that you
15   won't let me dance with your date?

16 MEG: She's not insecure, Darla!

17 DARLA: Sounds like it to me.

18 JAMIE: We just know that when you get your eyes fixed on
19   one of our dates, our night is over. All dressed up and
20   no date to be found!

21 DARLA: Oh, you're exaggerating!

22 TERESA: No, she's not. Remember the Fall Hayride?

23 DARLA: Uh, not really.

24 TERESA: Well, I do! My date, Brad, didn't even ride in the
25   same trailer as me! You pulled him into another one
26   with you!

27 DARLA: Oh, that.

28 JAMIE: And remember Homecoming?

29 DARLA: Not really.

30 JAMIE: There I was wearing this huge black and white
31   mum and my date, Stephen, forgot he was with me. You
32   two ran around underneath the bleachers the entire
33   game!

34 DARLA: Oh, that.

35 MEG: But tonight is going to be different, Darla.

1   DARLA: How's that, Miss-know-it-all?

2   MEG: Everyone keeps their own dates.

3   DARLA: Oh?

4   MEG: Ready, girls? *(Each girl pulls out a pair of handcuffs.)*

5   TERESA: And an extra pair for you, Darla. Aren't we nice?

6   DARLA: You've got to be kidding! I'm not handcuffing

7   myself to a boy!

8   TERESA: But Darla, it's the latest fad!

9   JAMIE: Haven't you heard about it?

10   MEG: Everybody's doing it!

11   DARLA: No way! I don't believe you.

12   JAMIE: Darla, would we lie to you?

13   DARLA: Probably.

14   TERESA: Oh, Darla, you can trust us! These handcuffs are

15   fun.

16   DARLA: Fun? You've got to be kidding!

17   MEG: It's true. This way you get to go everywhere with the

18   guy you're with.

19   JAMIE: Stick to his side all night long.

20   DARLA: I still don't believe you.

21   JAMIE: Darla, would we do it if it wasn't the latest thing?

22   TERESA: Darla! Who was it that opened your eyes to

23   wearing eyeliner on your lips?

24   DARLA: y'all did.

25   MEG: And who talked you into getting those awesome

26   shoes you're wearing?

27   DARLA: y'all did.

28   JAMIE: So ... what more can we say? Handcuffs are in!

29   DARLA: *(Accepting a pair)* Wow. Really? I didn't know. I

30   guess it could be fun. *(BRYAN, CHUCK, and MIKE enter.)*

31   BRYAN: Hello, you gorgeous girls!

32   CHUCK: Ready to rock and roll?

33   MIKE: Dance the night away?

34   BRYAN: Hey, Darla, you look hot!

35   DARLA: Thank you, Bryan!

1 JAMIE: Uh, Bryan. Do you like what *I'm* wearing?
2 BRYAN: Yeah, sure.
3 DARLA: Hey, Mike, do you prefer to dance fast or dance
4   slow? Actually, I like to dance slow. Hey, maybe we
5   could have a dance together.
6 MEG: Excuse me! Mind if I cut in? *(Steps between Mike and*
7   *Darla.)*
8 CHUCK: Hey, there's Coach Jenkins. Let's go say hi.
9 MIKE: We'll be right back, girls. *(Boys exit.)*
10 DARLA: Hey guys, wait up! I want to come with you! *(Runs*
11   *Off.)*
12 MEG: OK, girls, we've got to find Darla a date. And fast!
13 TERESA: Yeah, so she'll leave ours alone!
14 JAMIE: *(Looking around)* But who?
15 MEG: Who'd be dumb enough to get stuck with Darla?
16 JAMIE: There has to be somebody.
17 TERESA: I know! And I've got just the plan to do it! *(They*
18   *form a circle and talk quietly for a moment, then come*
19   *out laughing. They holler for MELVIN, the class nerd, to*
20   *come over.)*
21 MELVIN: *(Enters.)* What is it?
22 JAMIE: Melvin, we all want to dance with you tonight.
23 MELVIN: *(Shocked)* Me? But why?
24 MEG: But we keep fighting over who gets to dance with you
25   first.
26 JAMIE: So, that means you have to pick.
27 MELVIN: You're fighting over *me*?
28 TERESA: Melvin, you know we like you.
29 MELVIN: You do?
30 MEG: If only there were more of you to go around.
31 MELVIN: More of me? Is this a joke?
32 TERESA: Melvin, pick me! Dance with me first, OK? Please!
33 JAMIE: No, Melvin, pick me!
34 MEG: Hey, I spotted him first! So, I should get the first
35   dance!

1 TERESA: Says who? Melvin, pick me!

2 MELVIN: Wait a minute! Wait a minute! I can't even dance.

3 TERESA: Sure you can!

4 MELVIN: No, really, I can't. I just came here to play basketball
5   in the gym.

6 JAMIE: Oh, Melvin, you can dance! It's not hard. Come on,
7   we'll all practice and prove you wrong.

8 MELVIN: Uh ... I don't know.

9 MEG: Oh, come on, Melvin. You know, we really like you. And
10   we know you'd be good without even trying!

11 MELVIN: Really? *(Girls nod and circle around MELVIN and*
12   *start to dance. Slowly, as the girls encourage him, he begins*
13   *to dance. He dances very badly and the girls do everything*
14   *they can to keep from laughing. After a few minutes,*
15   *DARLA enters, watching them dance.)*

16 JAMIE: Doing great!

17 TERESA: Looking good!

18 MEG: What rhythm!

19 JAMIE: See, you are a great dancer, Melvin!

20 TERESA: You've definitely got some hot moves!

21 MEG: Even without any music.

22 DARLA: *(Bursts out laughing.)* You've got to be kidding!

23 JAMIE: So, Melvin, who gets the first dance?

24 TERESA: Me! Pick me!

25 MEG: No, me! Please, Melvin! Please!

26 MELVIN: Gosh, girls, it's hard to choose. I mean ... I never
27   thought ... I just don't know what to say!

28 JAMIE: I call it! I get the first dance!

29 TERESA: No, I want the first dance!

30 MEG: Excuse me, but so do I! I hope we get to have a slow
31   dance, Melvin.

32 DARLA: Oh, my gosh! I think I'm going to throw up!

33 JAMIE: Are we going to have to fight about this? Because I'm
34   ready!

35 DARLA: Wait a minute! Wait a minute! What is going on here?

1   Why in the world would you want to dance with *him*?

2   MEG: How can you even ask that?

3   DARLA: How can I ask that? He's the nerd of the century, and

4   you want to dance with him?

5   JAMIE: Darla, look at him! He's so adorable!

6   DARLA: *(Laughing)* Oh, right! Please!

7   TERESA: And he always says the cutest things!

8   MELVIN: *(Squirting nose spray into his nose)* **Ahhhh, that's**

9   better. I hate to be all stopped up. Especially when both

10   sides get plugged up and I have to breathe through my

11   mouth the whole time. But ahhhh ... that's much better.

12   TERESA: Oh, Melvin, you're so cute! *(BRYAN, CHUCK, and*

13   *MIKE enter.)*

14   MEG: And did you know that Melvin was elected to serve on the

15   new lunch program here at school?

16   MELVIN: *(Proudly)* President of the committee.

17   MIKE: Hey, I heard about that! It gives the kids a chance to have

18   a say in what's served in the cafeteria.

19   BRYAN: Melvin, you're the President?

20   MELVIN: Yes sir! That's me!

21   CHUCK: Hey, get rid of that Salisbury steak! Talk about

22   disgusting!

23   MIKE: And axe those instant potatoes!

24   MELVIN: *(Takes out a small notepad and pencil from his pocket.)*

25   I'll put those items at the top of my list. Any other ideas?

26   BRYAN: More pizza!

27   MIKE: Yeah, but loaded with meat! Not that cheese pizza!

28   CHUCK: Hey, how about steak and potatoes now and then? We

29   deserve it. We work hard.

30   BRYAN: Yeah!

31   MELVIN: *(Writing)* I don't see why not.

32   DARLA: And I wish the cafeteria would serve ice cream.

33   JAMIE: That's a good idea.

34   MEG: With more than one flavor!

35   TERESA: Yeah, like an ice cream parlor inside the school cafeteria!

1   MEG: Yeah!

2   DARLA: I love ice cream!

3   JAMIE: Melvin, do you think it would be possible?

4   MELVIN: Well ... I think so. Students and teachers could both

5   benefit from a small ice cream parlor in the cafeteria. And

6   as an added bonus, we could use students to serve the ice

7   cream, eliminating the need for extra cafeteria workers.

8   Ice cream is not too costly if bought in bulk. So no, I don't

9   see a problem with it at all. I will approach the committee

10   about it Monday morning.

11 BRYAN: Hey, cool!

12 MIKE: I wouldn't mind flopping ice cream into cones!

13 CHUCK: Yeah, that'd be fun!

14 TERESA: Oh, Melvin, you are so wonderful!

15 JAMIE: The best!

16 MEG: And have you decided who gets the first dance?

17 JAMIE: Me, me, me!

18 DARLA: Wait a minute, here! You girls already have dates! So, I

19   should get the first dance with Melvin!

20 TERESA: Well, you are right.

21 MEG: I guess it would be only fair.

22 JAMIE: I guess.

23 DARLA: So, Melvin, will you give me the first dance tonight?

24 MELVIN: Sure! I mean, gosh, who wouldn't want to dance with

25   the prettiest girl in the entire school?

26 DARLA: *(Giggling)* I know!

27 BRYAN: Hey, look! They opened the doors!

28 CHUCK: Let's go, girls!

29 MIKE: Come on! I'm ready to dance!

30 TERESA: Hey, you guys meet us inside, OK? We have to check

31   our makeup. *(Nodding, the boys exit.)* Hey, Melvin, wait!

32 MELVIN: What?

33 TERESA: Darla, did you tell Melvin about our cute new fad?

34 DARLA: Oh, the handcuffs! I almost forgot!

35 MEG: We're all doing it.

1   MELVIN: What about handcuffs?

2   JAMIE: It's the latest fad.

3   TERESA: *(Brings MELVIN and DARLA together and puts the*
4   *handcuffs on them.)* **This is so you'll enjoy the entire**
5   **evening together. Every dance. Melvin and Darla!**

6   MELVIN: Hey, this is cool! I'm stuck with Darla, the prettiest
7   girl in the entire school!

8   DARLA: *(Suddenly worried)* Uh ... When do we get them off?

9   JAMIE: When the dance is over.

10 TERESA: I have the key right here in my pocket. So after the
11   dance we'll meet back here, and I'll take them off.

12 MEG: Oh, the two of you look so cute together!

13 MELVIN: Come on, Darla! Let's go dance! And wait till you see
14   some of my cool moves! *(He pulls her away.)*

15 DARLA: Are y'all coming?

16 TERESA: We'll be right there! *(MELVIN pulls DARLA Off. The*
17   *girls look at each other, smile, and high five. They drop the*
18   *remaining handcuffs into a nearby trash can and exit,*
19   *laughing.)*

Photo by Barbara Peterson

About the Author

Laurie Allen is a West Texas playwright whose first play, *Gutter Girl*, won the Indian River Players Festival of One-Act Play Competition. She has participated in developing original one-act plays for Hood Junior High in Odessa, Texas. Her plays have been read and produced at The Gettysburg College, The Globe of the Great Southwest, and The Pasadena Little Theatre.

Allen's plays for teens have enjoyed wide success across the United States with many productions. She has had skits, duets, and plays published by various publishing companies. Many of her competition pieces have gone all the way to national speech and forensics competitions.

Her publications include *Comedy Duets for Teens, Two-Character Scenes for Teens, Comedy Duos For Teens, Comedy Scenes for Teens,* and *Comedy Duos For High School.*

Order Form

mp™

Meriwether Publishing Ltd.
PO Box 7710
Colorado Springs, CO 80933-7710
Phone: 800-937-5297 Fax: 719-594-9916
Website: www.meriwether.com

Please send me the following books:

_____ **Thirty Short Comedy Plays for Teens** $16.95
#BK-B292
by Laurie Allen
Plays for a variety of cast sizes

_____ **Make It Mystery #BK-B287** $19.95
by Craig Sodaro
An anthology of short mystery plays

_____ **On Stage! Short Plays for Acting Students** $16.95
#BK-B165
by Robert Mauro
24 short one-act plays for acting practice

_____ **Two Character Plays for Student Actors** $16.95
#BK-B174
by Robert Mauro
A collection of 15 one-act plays

_____ **Improv Ideas #BK-B283** $22.95
by Justine Jones and Mary Ann Kelley
A book of games and lists

_____ **Theatre Games for Young Performers** $16.95
#BK-B188
by Maria C. Novelly
Improvisations and exercises for developing acting skills

_____ **112 Acting Games #BK-B277** $17.95
by Gavin Levy
A comprehensive workbook of theatre games

**These and other fine Meriwether Publishing books are available at
your local bookstore or direct from the publisher. Prices subject to
change without notice. Check our website or call for current prices.**

Name: _____ e-mail: _____

Organization name: _____

Address: _____

City: _____ State: _____

Zip: _____ Phone: _____

❏ **Check enclosed**

❏ **Visa / MasterCard / Discover #** _____

Signature: _____ *Expiration
date:* _____ / _____
(required for credit card orders)

Colorado residents: Please add 3% sales tax.
Shipping: Include $3.95 for the first book and 75¢ for each additional book ordered.

❏ *Please send me a copy of your complete catalog of books and plays.*

Order Form

Meriwether Publishing Ltd.
PO Box 7710
Colorado Springs, CO 80933-7710
Phone: 800-937-5297 Fax: 719-594-9916
Website: www.meriwether.com

Please send me the following books:

_____ **Thirty Short Comedy Plays for Teens** $16.95
#BK-B292
by Laurie Allen
Plays for a variety of cast sizes

_____ **Make It Mystery #BK-B287** $19.95
by Craig Sodaro
An anthology of short mystery plays

_____ **On Stage! Short Plays for Acting Students** $16.95
#BK-B165
by Robert Mauro
24 short one-act plays for acting practice

_____ **Two Character Plays for Student Actors** $16.95
#BK-B174
by Robert Mauro
A collection of 15 one-act plays

_____ **Improv Ideas #BK-B283** $22.95
by Justine Jones and Mary Ann Kelley
A book of games and lists

_____ **Theatre Games for Young Performers** $16.95
#BK-B188
by Maria C. Novelly
Improvisations and exercises for developing acting skills

_____ **112 Acting Games #BK-B277** $17.95
by Gavin Levy
A comprehensive workbook of theatre games

These and other fine Meriwether Publishing books are available at
your local bookstore or direct from the publisher. Prices subject to
change without notice. Check our website or call for current prices.

Name: _____ e-mail: _____

Organization name: _____

Address: _____

City: _____ State: _____

Zip: _____ Phone: _____

❑ **Check enclosed**

❑ **Visa / MasterCard / Discover #** _____

Signature: _____ Expiration
date: _____ / _____
(required for credit card orders)

Colorado residents: Please add 3% sales tax.
Shipping: Include $3.95 for the first book and 75¢ for each additional book ordered.

❑ *Please send me a copy of your complete catalog of books and plays.*